DOUBLE-MINDED

How Sex Is Dividing the
Australian Church

MARK DURIE

db

DEROR BOOKS

Double-Minded:
How Sex is Dividing the Australian Church

Copyright 2023 © by Mark Durie
Published by Deror Books, Melbourne, Australia

deror**books**.com

ISBN: 978-1-923067-00-4

Apart from any fair dealing for the purposes of private study, research, criticism or review, no part of this work may be reproduced by electronic or other means without the permission of the publisher.

Cover design: Sayaka Miyashita
Cover image: *Jesus of Nazareth* by José Luis Castrillo – joseluiscastrillo.com

Contents

1. Introduction — 1
2. Is It All Really About Sex? — 7
3. Church Polities — 25
4. Denominations and Movements — 49
5. The Catholic Church — 63
6. The Anglican Church — 71
7. The Uniting Church — 89
8. Two Pentecostal Movements — 99
9. Two Reformed Denominations — 109
10. The State of the Churches — 119
11. Looking to the Future — 131

ACKNOWLEDGEMENTS

I am grateful to acknowledge the assistance of many who helped put this book together.

The idea for *Double-Minded* arose from the experience of preparing expert testimony for a 2020 Administrative Tribunal hearing in Perth, Western Australia. That hearing was about fostering rights, and whether the religious beliefs of a Christian couple about human sexuality made them unsuitable foster parents. I am grateful to John Steenhof, of the Human Rights Law Alliance, who commissioned that testimony and gave me cause to begin to flesh out the arguments which are developed further here.

I am also grateful for the support of the Institute of Spiritual Awareness, to all who read and commented on earlier drafts of part or all of the book, and to those who gave guidance in the book design process.

Mark Durie, October 2023.

ENDORSEMENTS

This highly accessible book reflects the deep scholarship and insights of its author. As we all seek to understand massive changes in our culture it superbly sets out the extraordinary divergence between modern and traditional Christian worldviews, which accounts for so much of the profound confusion that characterises our times.

– John Anderson, Former Deputy Prime Minister of Australia.

Mark Durie has provided a welcome resource on how Christians have reacted to the sexual revolution in our times. He covers the varied spectrum of Christian denominations and movements, so there is bad news and good news. While he writes calmly, describing a complex time of transition, we are confronted by the urgent question: Where do we go from here?

– Bishop Peter J. Elliott, Auxiliary Bishop Emeritus in Melbourne, and author of *The Sexual Revolution, History, Ideology, Power.*

This book is a masterly description of the rules and regulations of prominent Christian denominations in Australia. It reviews the sexual policies of these denominations, especially with regard to same-sex marriage, which became legal in Australia in 2017. This very useful text will enable its readers to assess relevant contemporary developments, for example, the push to adopt government-sponsored proposals to eliminate exemptions for independent religiously affiliated schools to hire people who adhere to and respect schools' ethos and values. This book describes how proponents of secularism seek to impose their preferred sexual ethical standards on Australia's religious groups. It also details the responses of religious denominations to these secular pressures. I strongly recommend this book to all people, progressives and conservatives alike, who are genuinely interested in the protection of religious freedom in Australia.

– Gabriël Moens, Emeritus Professor of Law, The University of Queensland.

Since the beginnings of the sexual revolutions of the 1960s, sex has assumed the centrality of a religion in Western sex-saturated societies. As Malcolm Muggeridge said, "Orgasm has replaced the cross … as the image of fulfilment". To accommodate the new morality some denominations have adjusted their doctrines in attempts to remain socially relevant, only to discover they are now spiritually irrelevant. The evidence is in their acceleration toward oblivion. Read Mark Durie's *Double-Minded* to discover what went wrong and how to avoid the death of your church.

– Stuart Robinson, Founding Pastor, Crossway Baptist.

Mark Durie has given us a great gift in combatting the religious illiteracy so prevalent in our world. He plainly and carefully outlines the Christian landscape in Australia with respect to how different church groups view human sexuality. With careful research and characteristic clarity, he makes the complicated simple and understandable to all. This will be a useful reference for those inside and outside the church alike as we navigate the future.

– Bishop Richard Condie, Anglican Diocese of Tasmania

1

INTRODUCTION

At the time of writing, Christian denominations across the West are dividing over differences in approaches to human sexuality. This is impacting Australia as well. This book explores how Christian churches in Australia are responding to this trend, and how varying forms of church governance influence how these divisions occur.

PARTING OF THE WAYS

George Yancey and Ashlee Quosigk, in *One Faith No Longer*, go so far as to suggest that the parting of the ways among Christians underway in North America is so profound that it will lead to two different religions. Whether this proves to be true or not, it is clear that divisions are impacting many different long-established denominations.

This is a global phenomenon. One example is a major division in progress in the United Methodist Church (UMC). This is a large global denomination centred in the United States, with around twelve million members worldwide.

Introduction

The UMC's official position on human sexuality has always been a conservative one: its *Book of Discipline* states that "not being celibate in singleness or not faithful in a heterosexual marriage" is a "chargeable offense". Furthermore, it states that "the practice of homosexuality ... [is] incompatible with Christian teaching" and that "self-avowed practicing homosexuals" cannot be ordained or appointed to serve as ministers in the Church. Despite this, if a jurisdiction within the denomination takes a different view of human sexuality, the denomination has found it has no effective mechanism to ensure conformity to the Church's policies. For example, when the Western Jurisdiction of the UMC voted in 2016 to appoint Karen Oliveto as the first openly gay UMC bishop—she is married to a UMC deaconess—the denomination was powerless to intervene.

After years of internal tensions over human sexuality, more than a thousand conservative UMC churches recently left the denomination. Many joined a new conservative denomination, the Global Methodist Church, which was founded in May 2022.

This UMC split is but one example among many, as an across-the-board realignment is being triggered by challenges to church doctrine and ethics in the aftermath of the sexual revolution.

This short book offers a road map for making sense of similar trends in the Australian context and anticipating the twists and turns that divisions are likely to take. Along the way, we will consider the particularities of Christian denominations and movements.

We will also consider some predictions, informed by global and local trends. The impact of this ideological divide on church health and decline is important for the future of Christianity in the West. I will offer suggestions about how the current divisions

INTRODUCTION

in Christian denominations will play out. I will also ask whether Christians who welcome the outcomes of the sexual revolution are on "the right side of history".

AUTHORITY AND DISCIPLINE

We will be considering **why** divisions between Christians have arisen over same-sex marriage. We will also examine **how** emerging divisions interact with differences in church governance and discipline, and the way in which Christian groups establish and preserve authority for their beliefs and practices.

> Who is on the right side of history?

This short book attempts to help readers understand where churches locate and construe authority for their particular beliefs and practices, and how they apply authority to impose discipline. We will look at why discipline is important, and to what extent churches have the ability or the will to ensure that their members adhere to their doctrines. These two considerations—where authority lies and how discipline is exercised—determine how denominations react to and manage the divisions they are facing.

RELIGIOUS LITERACY

This book has also been written to counter religious illiteracy. In late 2020, I was providing expert evidence in a Western Australian legal case concerning whether a Christian couple should be allowed to foster young children. The issue at hand was whether this couple's conservative religious beliefs about human sexuality made them unsafe for this role. In presenting my evidence, I discussed reports by NCLS Research, an Australian

INTRODUCTION

organisation that conducts the National Church Life Survey (NCLS) and publishes reports on the health of churches. During cross-examination, I was asked why NCLS Research didn't report on mosques, synagogues and temples. I found myself having to explain to the barrister that "church" refers to a Christian institution. Mosques, synagogues and temples are not churches but places of worship for Muslims, Jews, and Hindus respectively. This seemed a difficult concept for her to grasp. She was suffering from a severe, but not unusual, case of religious illiteracy.[1]

As secularism has now come to dominate public intellectual life in the West, Christians must also contend with widespread religious illiteracy. Secular commentators often do not understand Christians—their worldview, what motivates them, and how their institutions are structured. One reason for this is that the worldview of Christians is so different from, and indeed alien to, the dominant way of thinking in the surrounding culture, particularly in relation to the nature of the human person. To this lack of understanding can be added hostility towards the church's moral teachings. As Carl Trueman put it, "The old sexual codes of celibacy outside marriage and chastity within it are considered

> "The old sexual codes of celibacy outside marriage and chastity within it are considered ridiculous and oppressive."
>
> – Carl Trueman

---

[1] For engaging explorations of religious literacy, see the essays in Jenny Taylor. ed. 2016. *Religious Literacy: An Introduction*. London: Lapido Media.

ridiculous and oppressive, and their advocates wicked or stupid or both."[2]

Religious illiteracy affects people in different ways, depending on their backgrounds. It is not surprising that people tend to view Christianity from within the bubble of their own experience of church (or lack of it). Those who had some exposure to Christian faith as children, for example at a Christian school, may assume that all Christian expressions are similar to what they experienced. An ex-Catholic may assume that all Christian denominations are like the Catholic Church, with hierarchical authority structures. However, this is far from true, as we shall see.

Readers will not agree with everything written here, but my hope is that after reading this book, they will be informed and better able to understand, anticipate and trace the unfolding of the fragmentation of Christian denominations and movements. I hope that readers may be better able to interpret the times in which we find ourselves.

---

[2] Carl R. Trueman. 2020. *The Rise and Triumph of the Modern Self: Cultural Amnesia, Expressive Individualism, and the Road to Sexual Revolution.* Wheaton, IL: Crossway, p. 22.

2

IS IT ALL REALLY ABOUT SEX?

There are two opposing views about the refusal of some Christians to embrace the outcomes of the sexual revolution.

On the one hand, some argue that churches are increasingly out of step with progressive social trends and this is hastening their decline. By this view, conservative Christian views on sexual ethics are not only judgemental and regressive but, some would say, in conflict with Jesus' teachings on loving others. Best-selling author Nikki Gemmell, a self-professed Anglican, wrote in a weekly column for *The Weekend Australian,* entitled "Why the Anglican church must evolve or die",[3] that Anglicans who

> Do conservative sexual ethics conflict with Jesus' teaching on loving others?

---

3   Nikki Gemmell. "Why the Anglican Church must evolve or die." *The Australian*, 2 November 2019. theaustralian.com.au/weekend-australian-

reject same-sex marriage are "haters and bigots", on the "wrong side of public opinion", and slowly killing their denomination.

An opposing view is that the credibility of Christianity depends upon holding to a faith revealed to the apostles by Jesus Christ himself and passed on to churches through the Bible. Those who hold this view are quick to point out that Christianity did not get to where it is today—with over two billion adherents—by courting public opinion.

According to this second view, assimilating a church's beliefs with the sexual preferences of the age can only dilute the church's witness, condemning it to spiritual irrelevancy. As the Reverend Joshua Bovis put it in response to Gemmell, "If the church did what Ms Gemmell suggested, and mirrored the world, the church would be indistinguishable from the world and in essence have nothing to offer."[4]

Bovis has a point. As Jesus said, if salt becomes tasteless, the best thing is to get rid of it (Matthew 5:13). Why spend your Sunday mornings worshipping God and handing over your hard-earned cash if church merely offers what the ambient culture already provides? Or, as Daniel French put it, "We might as well have huge banners outside our church porches saying: 'Nothing worth seeing here.'"[5]

---

magazine/why-the-anglican-church-must-evolve-or-die/news-story/f3ac2d5f2bff96dedbbe8ea3b5275b64

[4] Joshua Bovis. "Engaging with the media—a worthwhile endeavour." *Anglican Church League*, 25 June 2021. acl.asn.au/engaging-with-the-media

[5] Daniel French. "Confessions of a woke vicar." *Conservative Woman*, 8 September 2023. www.conservativewoman.co.uk/thought-crimes-of-an-anti-woke-vicar/

DEEPER DRIVERS?

Many would agree with Nikki Gemmell that those who reject the outcomes of the sexual revolution, including same-sex marriage, are driven by hatred and bigotry. On the other hand, others point to deeper theological factors driving the divisions. Christian conservatives assert that the emerging divisions are fundamentally about the authority of the Bible, and whether the Bible or human reason will be the ultimate arbiter of faith and morals.

> The emerging divisions are about the authority of the Bible.

In his explanation for why he has left the United Methodist Church, Timothy Tennent writes of the "deeper malady, which is a growing disaffiliation from Scripture and from the historic witness of the church through the ages."[6]

The Global Anglican Future Conference (GAFCON) movement, which arose in response to North American Anglicans' embrace of same-sex marriage, has stated that the division is happening because some have "rejected God's written Word and have put their trust in their own reason":

> GAFCON is a Bible-based movement which submits to the authority of the Scripture. ... [Scripture] contains the key principles and teaching for mankind to be fully 'equipped' to live the way God wants.
>
> As well as the Bible, God has given humans reason and the historical witness of the church to discern matters of faith but GAFCON believe that Scripture is the higher authority.

---

6 Timothy Tennent. "Why I joined the Global Methodist Church." timothytennent.com/why-i-joined-the-global-methodist-church/

…

Sadly, there are those within the Anglican Communion, including whole Provinces, who have rejected the authority of God's written Word and have put their trust in their own reason. This has been most evident in the area of sexual ethics and human sexuality. And it is for this reason that GAFCON was formed; to restore the Bible to [the] heart of the Communion so that the Gospel of our Lord and Saviour Jesus Christ might not be compromised.[7]

In a similar vein, Cardinal George Pell, writing for *The Spectator* just before his death, objected that a booklet prepared in advance of an upcoming Roman Catholic "Synod on Synodality" was:

… hostile in significant ways to the apostolic tradition and nowhere acknowledges the New Testament as the Word of God, normative for all teaching on faith and morals. The Old Testament is ignored, patriarchy rejected and the Mosaic Law, including the Ten Commandments, is not acknowledged.[8]

For both GAFCON and Pell, a key issue facing the church of today is whether it will continue to uphold Biblical authority.

It is clear from the juxtaposition of the views of GAFCON with those of Cardinal George Pell that the battle within Christianity over Biblical authority transcends age-old Christian sectarian

> The battle within Christianity over Biblical authority transcends age-old Christian sectarian divisions.

---

7   gafcon.org/about/bible-based

8   George Pell. "The Catholic Church must free itself from this 'toxic nightmare'." *The Spectator*, 11 January 2023. spectator.co.uk/article/the-catholic-church-must-free-itself-from-this-toxic-nightmare

divisions. At its base, it is about a worldview conflict between secular Western culture and Biblical Christian culture.

WHAT DOES IT MEAN TO BE HUMAN?

One of the great issues of our age is the question of what it means to be human. As Andy Bannister has noted, it "is almost impossible to overstate how important this question is; it arguably lies behind every major ethical, cultural and political debate of our age."[9]

Carl R. Trueman has argued, in *The Rise and Triumph of the Modern Self*, that contemporary Western culture's embrace of the sexual revolution is grounded in a fundamental shift in understanding of what it means to be human, which has taken centuries to unfold and is now deeply embedded in the self-understanding of Western people.[10] It is proposed here that at the heart of the emerging divisions among Christians is a difference in understanding of what it means to be human. The issue is to what extent the dominant contemporary secular understanding of the human person should be allowed to reshape Christian ethics.

> The question of what it means to be human "lies behind every major ethical, cultural and political debate of our age."
> – Andy Bannister.

---

9 Andy Bannister. 2021. *Do Muslims and Christians Worship the Same God?* London: IVP, p. 78.

10 Carl R. Trueman. *The Rise and Triumph of the Modern Self*. A shorter, more accessible account of Trueman's argument is found in his 2022 book *Strange New World: How Thinkers and Activists Redefined Identity and Sparked the Sexual Revolution*. Wheaton, IL: Crossway.

A BIBLICAL VIEW

Christian tradition has always understood the teleology (or purpose) of the human in relation to the creator's purposes. As Lesslie Newbiggin put it,

> Human beings exist for God and for responsible relations with each other under God. The church is required to affirm this as public truth, which must govern public life even if it is contradicted by the majority.[11]

The point of being human—from a Biblical perspective—is to serve and worship God. This perspective projects an ethical framework which has shaped Christian thinking about morality. For example, it formed the Church of England's understanding of marriage, as enshrined in its marriage rite. The *Book of Common Prayer*, drawing upon the Bible, declares that the purpose of "holy matrimony", as ordained and instituted by the creator, is threefold. First, it was "ordained for the procreation of children" so that they can be brought up to worship and praise God. Second, it is a "remedy against sin and to avoid fornication", so that by

> Christians believe the purpose of being human is to serve and worship God.

the rightful meeting of sexual needs, both parties might "keep themselves undefiled members of Christ's body". Third, it is for "mutual society, help, and comfort". Note that the first two points are concerned with right worship: that children should be raised to worship God, and that married people should maintain themselves in holiness through avoiding sexual sin.

---

11 Lesslie Newbiggin. 1988. "Response to David M. Stowe." *International Bulletin of Mission Research*. 12(4):151–53.

This view of marriage is grounded in a theological and teleological understanding of the human person, which was once the dominant view in Western societies. However, this has been displaced by a materialistic and psychological conception of the human person.

EXPRESSIVE INDIVIDUALISM

The point of being human, according to the now dominant Western understanding, is to self-realise: it is to find happiness in fulfilling one's personal needs and psychological drives. Canadian philosopher Charles Taylor has called this received view of what it means to be human the *expressive individual*.[12]

The English cultural keywords *authenticity*, *fulfilment*, *agency*, *celebration*, and *identity* reflect this perspective. Today in Western societies, the point of being human is to be *authentically* oneself—to find *fulfilment* by living one's own life and no one else's. Individuals are supposed to have

> The "expressive individual" finds purpose in self-actualization.

agency, which means full control over their personal decisions. These attributes should be *celebrated* by others. The importance of celebration is captured in this statement about autistic people by social worker and spiritualist minister, Sharon Kaye-O'Connor:

> If we can … understand and meet the unique needs of autistic kids, while celebrating them for exactly who they are, we are

---

12 See Charles Taylor. 1989. *Sources of the Self: The Making of the Modern Identity*. Cambridge, MA: Harvard University Press, and Charles Taylor. 2007. *A Secular Age*. Cambridge, MA: Harvard University Press.

on track for raising happy, healthy, autistic people. And that's the ultimate goal.[13]

Our final keyword is *identity*. Someone's life has an essence, referred to as their identity. An individual should discern and determine this essence, whatever form it takes, and no one else has the right to tell them what that identity should be or how it should be realised.

Crucially, human identity has come to be understood as inherently sexual. The sexual understanding of identity has a history: the sexual revolution of the 1960s was preceded by two centuries of polemics against Christian understanding of the human person, including against Christian views of sexuality and marriage. This polemic was conducted by influential thinkers including Rousseau, Marx, Nietzsche and Freud.

> Human identity came to be understood as inherently sexual.

Expressive individualism is now so deeply embedded in Western cultures as to be beyond critique. It has become like the air we breathe. It dominates people's self-understanding and the way we talk about ourselves. At the same time, it is raising many important questions. One question is how our society is to respond to people who self-realise by identifying as a different gender from what their biology indicates. Should we consider the provision of puberty blocking drugs and gender-affirming surgery for children and young people to be a compassionate

---

13   Krystal Jagoo. "What's it like to be diagnosed with autism as an adult? New research takes a closer look." *VeryWellMind*, 16 January 2023. verywellmind.com/what-s-it-like-to-be-diagnosed-with-autism-as-an-adult-new-research-takes-a-closer-look-5203463

affirmation of young people's self-identification, or medical abuse of vulnerable minors?

The questions that expressive individualism poses for our society are not limited to the domains of sexuality and gender. For example, in race relations, questions arise about what to make of people who identify as indigenous although all their ancestors were white European immigrants. Are such people to be celebrated as quintessential examples of courageous self-realisation, or rejected as rent-seeking frauds?

> The questions expressive individualism poses are not limited to sexuality and gender.

Questions also arise in relation to reports of falling literacy levels among young people. Many schoolteachers now see themselves as enablers of student learning rather than as experts with skills, knowledge, and truths to impart. English teacher Conor Ross reports that he "was given the impression that English teaching … is, above all else, about facilitating the self-expression of our students." Ross quotes Melbourne University School of Education academic Ray Misson:

> English teachers are not on about teaching single truths, they are on about capacity building, giving students the capacity to create their own set of values and their own hierarchy of truths …[14]

Is this change in understanding of education to be celebrated as liberating students in their quest for self-realisation, or is it a betrayal of children's need and right to be taught?

14   Ray Misson. 2006. "Connecting with the world of texts." *Idiom* 42:6.

One of the challenges of expressive individualism is the valorising of particular identities which are considered to have been inhibited by the unjust use of power—in other words, to have been oppressed—and the stigmatisation of those who are considered to belong to the class of oppressors. Society can be blind to the plight of some while exaggerating the plight of others. It becomes acceptable to publicly abuse some people while displaying extreme sensitivity and deference to others. There is now a hierarchy of acceptable and unacceptable victimhoods. For example, it is difficult to acknowledge the existence of Christians who are persecuted and discriminated against in a culture in which the label "Christian" has been linked to oppressiveness and in which the struggle against Christian morality has been at the core of the ideology of the expressive self.

> There is now a hierarchy of acceptable and unacceptable victimhoods.

More generally, the mindset of expressive individualism faces a number of challenges, including how to account for the human propensity to cause harm, and how to set safe limits around individual self-realisation. To embrace expressive individualism as inherently good requires an act of faith in human nature: it requires a belief that the human self is always good, for it is this belief that makes it possible to see self-determination as good. For self-determination to be good, the self itself must be good. But how, then, do we account for the fact that there have always been people who abuse others to achieve their own ends? Expressive individualism also raises a related question: How can an individual know that they are a good person who does what is right?

These dynamics play out, for example, in the medical treatment of transgender youth. If a young person declares that they wish to identify as a gender that is different from their biology, a medical professional may be inclined to see this act of self-determination as inherently good. In this way, health professionals may refuse to entertain the possibility that transitioning could be a form of

> "They feel like really good people because they're being inclusive."
>
> – Dr Jillian Spencer

self-harm rather than a liberating act of self-realisation. Health professionals can feel good about themselves for promoting the young person's expressive self: they are being "inclusive". Queensland child psychiatrist Jillian Spencer describes the dilemma that parents face:

> It will suddenly dawn on you (you) are not in with a chance to protect your child. These people you are relying on for help in the village it takes to raise a child are not actually interested in the long-term welfare of your child. They don't suffer if your child becomes infertile or never experiences sexual pleasure or lives with debilitating side-effects from puberty blockers and cross-sex hormones.
>
> But they feel like really good people because they're being inclusive.[15]

If the expressive individual's drive to self-realisation is seen as morally pristine, this raises the deeper question of where to locate all the harm in our world. Where does evil come from? The Biblical

---

15 Natasha Robinson. "Senior child psychiatrist stood down after questioning gender medicine." *The Weekend Australian*, 10 June 2023. theaustralian.com.au/nation/senior-child-psychiatrist-stood-down-after-questioning-gender-medicine/news-story/b418333aa19de951acb98601bf4ca31d

view is that good and bad are both woven into the structure of the human soul. Aleksandr Solzhenitsyn put it like this:

> In the intoxication of youthful successes I had felt myself to be infallible, and I was therefore cruel. In the surfeit of power I was a murderer, and an oppressor. In my most evil moments I was convinced that I was doing good, and I was well supplied with systematic arguments. And it was only when I lay there on rotting prison straw that I sensed within myself the first stirrings of good. Gradually it was disclosed to me that the line separating good and evil passes not through states, nor between classes, nor between political parties either—but right through every human heart—and through all human hearts.[16]

> "The line separating good and evil runs through every human heart."
> – Aleksandr Solzhenitsyn

In contrast, the dominant view of the past two centuries, reflected in the emergence of the expressive self, is that it is society's institutions that can be wrong or bad, not people, and the source of harm is to be found in the limitations that those institutions place on individuals, which prevent them from fully realising themselves: there are no bad people as such, only bad social structures. By this view, there is no point to the Christian concept of individual salvation, because there is nothing that the human person needs to be saved from.[17]

---

16 Aleksandr Isayevich Solzhenitsyn. 1975. *The Gulag Archipelago 1918–1956*. Trans. T. P. Whitney. New York: Harper & Row, p. 25.

17 Strikingly, Islamic teaching agrees. As the Palestinian–American philosopher Isma'il al-Faruqi put it, "Man stands in no predicament from which he is to be 'saved'." Isma'il Raji al-Faruqi. 2000. *Al Tawhid:*

IS IT ALL REALLY ABOUT SEX?

To this can be added a crucial caveat: that people who stand for harmful institutions can be considered tarred by the brush of institutional evil. In Australia, individuals who have been admitted to this category by the court of public opinion include former Australian Prime Minister Scott Morrison and Cardinal George Pell. Some would also insist that certain whole groups of people—for example, white males—are tainted with institutional evil.

All this echoes Rousseau's idea that the natural state of the human self is morally pristine.

If evil is indeed structural, then the liberating battle for human self-expression must be waged within the institutions. Consequently, the expressive individual is inherently suspicious of institutions.

> The expressive individual is inherently suspicious of institutions.

Another problematic implication of expressive individualism is the alienation of the psychological self from the body—seen, for example, in a trans identity which conflicts with the sexual attributes of a physical body.

Yet another cost of this way of viewing human beings is social disconnection. For the inward-looking self, social and moral obligations to others are potentially threatening and harmful. The inward turn comes at a cost to wider society, as social virtues such as gratitude, humility, honesty, duty, vocation, and service are questioned and disdained because they threaten to constrain

---

Its Implications for Thought and Life. Herndon, VA: International Institute of Islamic Thought, p. 72.

and limit individual self-realisation, even though they may bring demonstrable benefits to society as a whole.

What is crucial for our purposes is that the ideology of the self-realising person impacts how the institutions of marriage and the family are viewed. For the expressive individual, marriage should serve as a vehicle for individual self-realisation, and divorce can be seen as a liberating corrective act which allows people to continue to realise themselves freely without the restraints imposed by a marriage contract.

> The sexual revolution placed sex at the heart of personal identity.

The sexual revolution unshackled the expressive individual's sexuality from the constraints of the social contract of marriage and the limitations of biology, while placing sex at the heart of personal identity. As Trueman has pointed out, this is the legacy of Sigmund Freud, who taught that much of what it means to be humans is about sex. A person's sexual activity was, for Freud, not just something they did, but an expression and reflection of their deepest identity. It was Freud who invented the idea of sexual orientation as an inherent attribute of the self. As Michel Foucault put it:

> The nineteenth-century homosexual became a personage, a past, a case history, and a childhood, in addition to being a type of life, a life form and a morphology ... The sodomite had been a temporary aberration; the homosexual was now a species.[18]

---

18   Michel Foucault. 1978. *The History of Sexuality.* Vol.1. Trans. Robert Hurley. New York, NY: Pantheon Books, p. 43. Foucault himself regretted this conflation of identity and sexual practice.

IS IT ALL REALLY ABOUT SEX?

The sexual revolution of the 1960s was a key point when this Western psychological understanding of the sexual self broke through to establish its dominance in Western cultures. Pop music spread the self-love. Thus the hook from the song *Because I love you*, released in 1970 by the Masters Apprentices, told listeners to do what they want to do and be what they want to be.

Turbocharged by technology—the pill, abortion, mass media, and advertising—this sexualised, self-expressive understanding of what it means to be human has colonised and transformed Western culture's understanding of the value of the human person.

By this view, to deny marriage to people who do not fulfil a Biblical understanding of marriage is hateful, because it denies someone the right to realise themselves by fulfilling their sexual identity. It stops people from being freely and authentically themselves and denies them the celebration that their self-realisation deserves.

For centuries, advocates of the liberation of people from the restraints of the Christian religion have been making their vigorous opposition to Biblical sexual ethics known. The now dominant understanding of the human person as a self-realising sexual being contrasts profoundly with a Biblical view of human beings made in the image of God, owing obedience and worship to their creator and constrained by the creator's laws.

> The idea of the self-realizing sexual person contrasts with the Biblical understanding of people made in the image of God.

A challenge for the church is that the all-pervasive idea of the expressive self has also impacted Christians. The emerging

21

divisions in Western Christian denominations reflect a tension between expressive individualism and a conservative Biblical understanding of human identity. All in the West have had their thinking and outlook shaped by expressive individualism. Disagreements arise over where to draw the theological lines and how much a Biblical anthropology can be made to accommodate the expressive individualism of our age.

This is a very deep divide indeed. It is not fundamentally about sex (or gender) at all. It is about the whole point of being human. The emerging fracturing of churches is about who we are as people, and whether a Biblical worldview can accommodate a radical shift in understanding of what it means to be human.

> The division among Christians is about the whole point of being human.

CHRISTIAN RESPONSES

The question is not whether Christianity should be influenced by the surrounding culture, for that is inevitable. The question is where a line is to be drawn between reasonable cultural accommodation and the subversion of church doctrine and ethics.

Christian advocates for same-sex marriage argue that there can be an accommodation. They propose, first, that the Bible's negative judgements of same-sex relationships do not address the issue of loving same-sex relationships at all, but are in fact about issues like sexual violence and exploitation. Second, they argue that same-sex relationships can and must be embraced, to the extent that they are loving, on the basis of the Bible's call to love others.[19]

It needs to be understood that the struggles over human sexuality are played out at two levels. On one level, there are theologians and religious teachers slugging it out to establish the rightness of their views. On another level, deep cultural shifts are affecting church members, manifested in changing attitudes to sexual expressions as well as changing patterns of behaviour. In a sense, the theologians are trying to sort things out after the sexual revolution cultural tsunami has already swept through the churches.

One piece of evidence for the explanation being offered here is that there is a correlation, as we shall see, between acceptance by Christians of same-sex marriage and acceptance of sex outside and before marriage. As church divisions continue to progress, it is becoming clearer that Christians who embrace same-sex marriage are also more accepting—not inevitably, but on the whole—of sex outside marriage: the embrace of homosexual marriage goes hand-in-hand with acceptance of adultery and fornication. I am not saying that someone who advocates for same-sex marriage will necessarily be more embracing of adultery and fornication. The level of acceptance of these practices varies a great deal between individuals, and it is common for people to be more liberal on one issue (for example,

> Christians who embrace same-sex marriage are also more accepting of sex outside marriage.

---

19 For a variety of theological views held by Christians on same-sex marriage, see the essays in Anglican Church of Australia Doctrine Panel. 2019. *Marriage, Same-Sex Marriage and the Anglican Church of Australia: Essays from the Doctrine Commission.* Mulgrave: Broughton.

fornication) and less liberal on another (for example, adultery). My point is that, overall, the trend is that churches whose members hold more liberal views on homosexuality will also have more liberal views on other aspects of human sexuality.[20]

The ideological inconsistency in embracing same-sex marriage while rejecting adultery is that prohibitions against both of these conflict with expressive individualism. The cultural driver is the pursuit of individuals' freedom to express their sexual identities with authenticity in whatever way they feel is best for their self-realisation. Ultimately, expressive individualism demands the rejection, stigmatisation, and cancelling of moral categories such as fornication and adultery.

> Expressive individualism demands the rejection of the moral categories of fornication and adultery.

A second piece of evidence for the explanation being offered here is that the majority of contexts in which Christians are dividing over the issue of human sexuality are in the West. This is because it is mainly in the West that the self-realising individual has become the dominant way of thinking about what it means to be human.

---

20 There is also a trend for Christian advocates of sexual progressivism to be theologically liberal. This is a large and complex topic, which goes beyond the scope of this book. I offer just one example. In 2023, a new Anglican Archbishop of Brisbane, Jeremy Greaves, was elected. Archbishop Greaves is an outspoken supporter of same-sex marriage. When asked by Rachael Kohn, on the ABC's *The Spirit of Things*, "Do you specifically then have difficulties with the Apostles' Creed that you might like to rewrite it or ditch it?" Greaves responded, "I'd be happy to abandon the Creed." abc.net.au/listen/programs/spiritofthings/progressive-christianity-pt-2/3101788

3

CHURCH POLITIES

Today, there are around 2.4 billion Christians in the world, constituting one-third of the world's population.[21] But what do these people have in common? What is Christianity?

Christianity developed from a movement that arose among the followers of Jesus of Nazareth two thousand years ago. Those followers believed that Jesus was both the "Son of God" and God incarnate, who preached a message—referred to as the *gospel*—about the reign of God, performed miracles, healed the sick, freed people suffering from evil spirits, was crucified by the Roman authorities, was raised to life again, ascended into heaven, reigns now over all things, and will come again to judge all people. Christians believe that there is life after death and that all will face judgement for what they have done in the one life they have to live.

> What is Christianity?

The core source and authority for these and other Christian beliefs is the Bible, a collection of 66 books. This is divided into

---

[21] In 2011, the Pew Research Center put the total number of Christians at 2.18 billion. pewforum.org/2011/12/19/global-christianity-exec

two parts. Thirty-nine books make up the Old Testament, which is also the Jewish Bible and is written mainly in the Hebrew language with some parts in Aramaic. Twenty-seven books make up the New Testament, which is in Greek. Most Christians believe that the New Testament faithfully reports the teachings of Jesus and his immediate followers, known as the *apostles*.

> The Bible projects a transcendant worldview, with a particular understanding of what it means to be human.

The Bible projects a transcendent worldview, including a particular understanding of what it means to be human, the essential problems humans face in this life, and how people can address these problems with God's help, including a God-given system of ethics.

CHRISTIAN GROUPS AND DENOMINATIONS

Christians belong to a wide variety of movements, organised in diverse ways. Some, but not all, of these movements are known as "denominations".

A basic universal building block of Christian communities is the local congregation. It is above the congregation level that we may encounter denominations.

The word *denomination*, which originally meant 'naming', implies the existence of an accepted, official name for an association of congregations, and a formally established internal polity, which includes a process for recognising or licensing pastors and other leaders as well as criteria for individuals and congregations to be considered members of the denomination. Denominations also have a formally articulated set of doctrines.

The official names of denominations are derived in different ways. Some refer to the name of a founder, such as *Lutheran* after Martin Luther (d. 1546), *Calvinist* after John Calvin (d. 1564), and *Wesleyan* after John Wesley (d. 1791). Others refer to a nation or ethnicity, such as *Church of England*, *Anglican* (also referring to England), *Roman*, and *Coptic*, which means 'Egyptian'. Some denominational titles refer to theological traditions, such as *Reformed*, *Catholic*, *Pentecostal*, and *Orthodox*. Others refer to practices, such as *Baptist* (which signals rejection of infant baptism and affirmation of adult believer's baptism by full immersion) and *Methodist* (which refers to the methodical way in which the Wesleyan movement was organised). Still other names refer to a mode of governance, such as *Episcopalian* and *Presbyterian*. Some names combine different kinds of labels—for example, *Greek Orthodox*.

Names can tell us about the history of a denomination. An example of a more complex denominational title is the *Free Reformed Churches of Australia* (FRCA). The term *Reformed* identifies with Calvinist Protestant tradition. The term *free* in Protestant contexts often refers to a theological commitment concerning church governance, namely that a church is separate from the state. Thus, in Germany, churches called *frei* are Protestant but not part of the established state church system. However, the term *Free* in the case of the FRCA is a reference to a conservative reform movement in Holland in 1944, known as the *vrijmaking* ('making free'). The FRCA was founded in the post-war period by supporters of the *vrijmaking* movement who had emigrated to Australia and chose not to join with other

Reformed believers. They wished to remain "free", to stay true to the reform principles of 1944.

It must be emphasised that not all Christian groups that could be called a *denomination*, as defined above, accept this label. For example, the Roman Catholic Church does not consider itself to be a denomination, but the original one true universal church of Jesus Christ.

At the other end of the spectrum, movements with a congregational model of governance, in which authority derives from the local congregation, also do not like to refer to themselves as denominations. An example is the Australian Baptists, who describe themselves on their website not as a denomination but as a "movement".[22] This is also the self-understanding of Australian Christian Churches (ACC), formerly known as the Assemblies of God. The ACC website describes itself as a:

> Baptists describe themselves, not as a denomination, but as a "movement".

> movement of Pentecostal churches in voluntary cooperation. Each individual church is self-governing, but commits itself to work together with other churches in the movement for the purpose of mutual support and the spread of the gospel in Australia and the world.[23]

Some congregational churches function as denominations in their own right, each congregation determining its own doctrine,

---

22 baptist.org.au/about-us

23 acc.org.au/about-us

governance, requirements for membership, and affiliation with other Christian groups.

Some Protestant congregations describe themselves as "non-denominational". In the United States, non-denominational churches, taken together, represent the third-largest Christian category in the nation after the Roman Catholic Church and the Southern Baptist Convention. There are also many non-denominational congregations in Australia, but they are not as large a slice of the Christian pie as in America.

It can be helpful to keep in mind that some terms can do double duty, being used to refer to broader groupings as well as to denominations. For example, *Anglican* can refer to a worldwide family of national and regional denominations that align themselves to a tradition founded in the Church of England. At the same time, this label can also appear in the name of a specific denomination—for example the *Anglican Church of Australia*. The label *Baptist* can refer to a particular set of beliefs or family of denominations, and the same label can also appear in the names of movements or denominations, such as the *Southern Baptist Convention*. The *Handbook of Denominations in the United States* identifies 26 Baptist groups, each of which is an independent denomination with the word *Baptist* in its name.[24]

THE PROBLEMATIC TERM "RELIGION"

The Australian Census form provides a list of "religions" which includes the names of some Christian denominations and asks

---

24 Roger E. Olson, Frank S. Mead, Samuel S. Hill, and Craig D Atwood. 2018. *Handbook of Denominations in the United States*. 14th edition. Nashville, TN: Abingdon Press.

people to nominate their "religion" from the list. However, this is not how most active Christians use the term "religion".

Christians do not normally refer to their denomination—if they have one—as their "religion". For example, an active involvement in an Anglican church will normally foster the belief that one's religion is Christianity, not Anglicanism. If active Australian Anglican churchgoers are asked what their religion is, most would simply say "Christian". It is "nominals"—people who rarely or never attend church, but still identify in some sense as having a denominational identity—who tend to refer to the denominational label as their "religion". If you asked someone "What's your religion?" and they said "Anglican", this would suggest that they rarely go to church and do not practice their faith.

> Christians do not normally refer to their denomination as their "religion".

The Australian Census notwithstanding, most Australian Christians would simply describe their religion as "Christian". Nevertheless, there is a sense in which there is no one Christian religion, so if one wanted to determine what the doctrine of a particular believer's religion was, the pertinent answer could be a combination of their individual belief system, the doctrine of their local congregation, and the doctrine of their denomination.

LEGAL IMPLICATIONS

These reflections can have legal implications. Australian anti-discrimination laws, when referring to the beliefs and practices of religious people, typically refer to a "religion". For example, anti-discrimination laws may include exemptions for actions "conducted in accordance with the doctrines, tenets, beliefs or teachings of a particular religion".[25] When the application of these laws is teased out in courts and tribunals, it can be tricky to work out exactly what a "particular religion" consists of, and who speaks for it.

> It can be tricky to work out what a particular religion is, and who speaks for it.

This has been a disputed point in anti-discrimination cases. The Sydney Wesley Mission Council (WMC) in Sydney, part of the Uniting Church, found itself involved in a complaint that they had wrongfully discriminated against a homosexual couple who wished to become foster carers. The WMC had rejected the couple's application, claiming a religious exemption. A key issue was whether "the religion" was that of the WMC, the Uniting Church, or Christianity itself. Initially, the Tribunal found that "the religion" in question was the "religion of Christianity". This opened the door for the Tribunal to heed expert evidence that the "religion of Christianity" does not support discrimination against homosexual people. However, the WMC successfully appealed this finding on the grounds that their religion was neither Christianity nor that of the Uniting Church, but "Wesleyanism", a variety of evangelical Christianity with stricter sexual ethics.

An argument can be made that to allow for full freedom of religion, an individual should be able to claim in a court of law that their individual belief system can be their "religion"; however, courts tend to look to written authorities to determine what the doctrine of a person's "religion" is. This was the case in *Christian Youth Camps Ltd v Cobaw Community Health*

---

25 See Section 38 of the federal *Sex Discrimination Act 1984*.

Services Ltd, when a Brethren Church camping ministry was successfully sued for rejecting a booking for a group of same-sex attracted youth. In the initial hearing of the case at the Victorian Civil and Administrative Tribunal, Judge Hampel ruled that it is not personal religious beliefs that are protected by religious exemptions, but the doctrines of a religion, which she took to be those written statements accepted by the religion as doctrines and to which the denomination expects conformity. She was guided in this decision by expert testimony from a Uniting Church theologian, Dr Rufus Black. Christian Youth Camps was at a disadvantage because the Brethren Church characteristically follows no written creed and does not have a formal statement of its doctrines and ethics.

> The word "religion" is problematic.

How to define "the religion" of litigants in anti-discrimination cases remains a messy area of law, with a gap between how lawyers and courts work on the one hand and how religious belief actually works in the real world on the other. A key issue is the problematic nature of the word "religion", and whether laws protecting freedom of religion should protect people's actually held religious beliefs or the "doctrines" of formal, organised religions.

As we shall see, the extent to which a denomination or movement commits its beliefs to writing varies considerably. The effect of this could be that those "religions" that have more detailed formal doctrinal statements will gain more protection for the religious freedoms of their adherents in Australian courts.

> Should religious freedom laws protect actual personal beliefs, or the doctrines of formal religion?

Another area in which clarity is lacking is the status of church codes of conduct. Some of the provisions of these codes, such as prohibitions of unchastity and adultery, are clearly based on religious beliefs, but it is far from clear—even though they are committed to writing and ministers are required to agree to conform to them—whether a secular court will consider the beliefs guiding such prohibitions to be protected as doctrines of the religion.

Whether sexual ethics are part of religious doctrine is at present one of the points of dispute in denominations that are dividing. Some, who would embrace same-sex marriage, say they are not, therefore introducing same-sex marriage is not a doctrinal innovation; others, who reject same-sex marriage, say that sexual ethics are part of doctrine.

DENOMINATIONAL POLITY

A key issue in understanding how churches are responding to the impact of the sexual revolution on the surrounding culture is the way Christian groups and individuals establish the authority for their beliefs. Who has authority to speak for or determine the doctrine or beliefs of a denomination? This depends upon the denomination's polity and how it is structured.

> The way authority works in churches varies greatly.

It is often not well understood that the way authority works varies greatly across different Christian traditions. This is true of both doctrine and administration.

Congregations in the Baptist and Pentecostal traditions are normally self-regulating. Self-regulating congregations, even though they may be affiliated with larger movements, function on their own authority. Such congregations can easily change

> There are three main models of polity in churches: episcopal, presbyterian, and congregational.

their affiliation, leaving one affiliation and joining another, or they may decide to declare their independence. For example, in 2018, Australia's largest church, Hillsong, left the Australian Christian Churches movement to set up its own global movement.

On the other hand, the Christian movements known as "denominations" typically look to historical defining documents, such as creeds and catechisms, for their doctrinal authority.

There are three main models of church polity found in Australian churches: *episcopal*, *presbyterian*, and *congregational*, each of which is defended by its adherents on Biblical grounds.

EPISCOPAL POLITY

For denominations with an episcopal tradition, the source of authority is the bishop, who presides over a geographical region known as a diocese. This is the most ancient form of Christian church polity.

The word *bishop* is derived from the Greek word *episkopos* ('overseer'), which is mentioned in the New Testament letters as one of the leadership roles in young churches. In the early church, the custom developed that each major city would have an *episkopos* who headed the Christian congregations in the city and surrounding country.

According to ancient custom, in episcopal denominations, bishops are considered to be "successors to the apostles, the chief teacher in every diocese, and the focus of local unity for their people".[26] They are expected to exert influence in guiding the faithful within their diocese. They are the pastor to their whole diocese, with the clergy functioning, in a sense, as their assistants, working under their licence and by their permission.

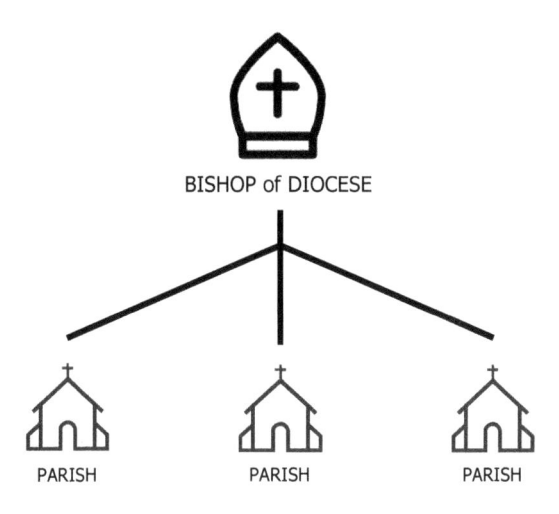

BISHOP of DIOCESE

PARISH   PARISH   PARISH

Episcopal Polity

In episcopal denominations, in keeping with ancient tradition, bishops normally have tenured appointments, which continue until their retirement or death.

Archbishop is simply the title given to the bishop of a major metropolitan diocese. In the Australian Anglican Church, this is the ex-officio title of the diocesan bishops of Brisbane, Sydney, Melbourne, Adelaide, and Perth. The Australian Catholic

---

26 George Pell. "The Catholic Church must free itself from this 'toxic nightmare'."

Church also has Archbishops for these five cities, plus Canberra and Hobart.

Within a particular episcopal tradition, dioceses may affiliate with other dioceses to form what Anglicans call a *province*. For example, the 23 Anglican dioceses in Australia have entered into a union with each other. The resulting body, the Australian Anglican Church (AAC), is regulated by a General Synod: a national Anglican parliament for lay people and clergy from across Australia which meets every five years.

The AAC is not a top-down hierarchy; it is more like a consortium. Determinations of the General Synod become binding in an individual diocese only after they are ratified by that diocese, and changes to the Constitution of the AAC can only be implemented if they are endorsed by every single one of the 23 dioceses. In the end, real authority rests with the individual dioceses, not with the province.

The AAC is, in turn, part of a larger consortium: the global Anglican Communion. The bishops of this communion have traditionally met at Lambeth in England every ten years, in a convocation invited and led by the Archbishop of Canterbury. Lambeth does pass resolutions; however, as with the Australian General Synod's determinations, these resolutions are not binding on the provinces or the dioceses.

In Australian Anglican dioceses, the appointment of diocesan bishops is done at the diocesan level, either by an election of the Synod of the diocese, which is a governing body of clergy and lay people, or by a board of electors appointed by the Synod.

> In an Anglican system, the diocesan bishop is the source of authority.

The Anglican situation is complex, but a core principle is that the diocese, with its bishop, is the principal constituting unit of authority. It is the diocesan bishop who ordains ministers, and all ministries exercised in a diocese must be licensed by the bishop. This means that the bishop can exercise significant control over the doctrine taught in their diocese.[27] Anglicans are not compelled to accept what their bishop teaches, but the bishop can determine who ministers in their diocese, and by this means they can exert influence to establish doctrinal uniformity. For Australian Anglicans, what this boils down to is that for the issue of same-sex marriage, 23 distinct dioceses with their bishops will ultimately each need to make their own determinations on the issue. There is not one decision about marriage for Australian Anglicans to make, but 23 decisions, each determined by a diocesan bishop in consultation with the lay and clergy members of their diocese.

> For Australian Anglicans, there is not one decision to make about same-sex marriage, but 23 decisions— one for each diocese.

The Catholic episcopal system in Australia is more complex than the Anglican system, with a number of ethnic dioceses with their own bishops alongside the regional dioceses. These ethnic divisions, known as *eparchies*, cover the Eastern branches of Catholicism, including Maronites, Ukrainian Greek Catholics,

---

27 See *Outline of the Structure of the Anglican Church of Australia*, a report submitted by General Synod to the Royal Commission into Church Abuse. childabuseroyalcommission.gov.au/sites/default/files/ANG.0017.001.0001_0.pdf

Melkites, Syro-Malabar Catholics and Chaldean Catholics. The eparchies all report directly to Rome.

Some episcopal denominations, such as the Coptic Church or Catholic Church, are led by a patriarch or pope, who has oversight over the appointment of diocesan bishops. However, even in the Catholic Church, diocesan bishops have a considerable degree of autonomy, and the Pope can only remove bishops from office under rare and unusual circumstances.

PRESBYTERIAN POLITY

In a presbyterian model of church polity, church governance is in the hands of an assembly of senior members of congregations, known as presbyters, a word which comes from the New Testament Greek word *presbyteros* ('elder').[28]

In churches with presbyterian polity, not all elders are known as "ministers": this title is usually reserved for designated teaching elders.

Presbyterian polity applies first of all at the level of the local congregation, which is governed by a church council or *session*. Congregations may then be grouped together in a region and function under the covering of a *presbytery* or *classis*, which is a higher representative assembly. Presbyteries may be further grouped under a general Assembly. In this way, the principle of assemblies is applied across multiple levels, with higher levels having authority over lower levels.

Authority in a presbyterian system, both doctrinal and administrative, derives from the higher gatherings. For

---

28 The English word *priest* comes from *presbyteros*.

example, it is the presbytery that ordains and licenses pastors of local congregations.

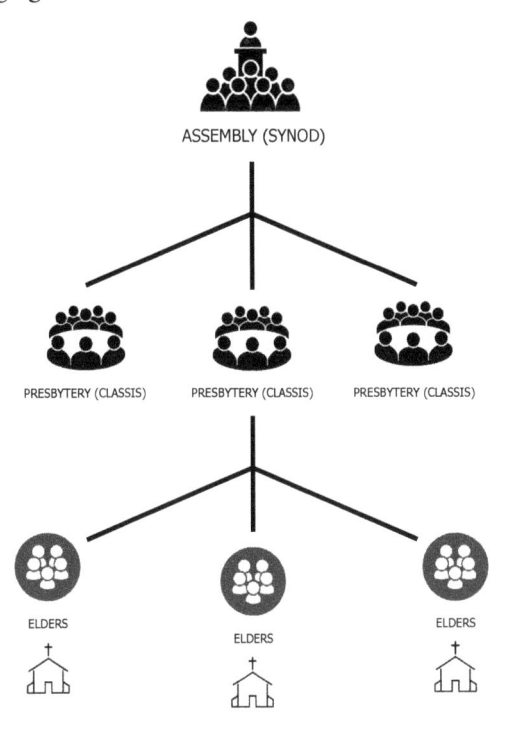

ASSEMBLY (SYNOD)

PRESBYTERY (CLASSIS)   PRESBYTERY (CLASSIS)   PRESBYTERY (CLASSIS)

ELDERS   ELDERS   ELDERS

Presbyterian Polity

In a presbyterian system, unlike the episcopal system, authority does not reside in an individual office but in the whole assembly. Higher assemblies are chaired by elected officials, who typically only hold office for limited terms, not unlimited terms as in episcopal systems. For example, the chair of the General Assembly of the Presbyterian Church of Australia is known as

> In a presbyterian system, authority derives from the higher gatherings.

a *Moderator* and holds office for three years. At a lower level, Australian Presbyterian state assemblies appoint Moderators for one-year terms.

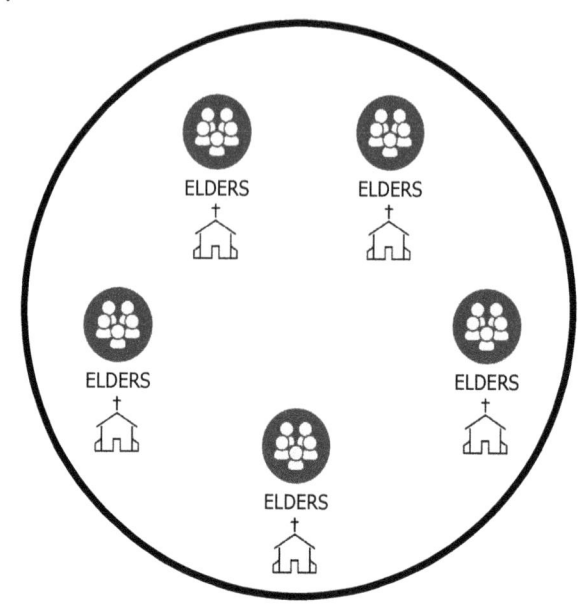

CONGREGATIONAL POLITY

In a congregational polity, the local congregation exercises full authority over itself, normally through a board of elders. It is, in a sense, its own denomination, and it determines its own doctrine and order.

Congregational Polity

Congregational churches can be fully independent, but many are affiliated into larger associations of churches. This affiliation is typically framed by a doctrinal consensus, expressed in a formal document or covenant, which member churches and leaders agree to, and also by other conditions of participation in the movement,

> In a congregational polity, the local congregation exercises authority over itself.

such as a code of conduct for ministers. Affiliation with a larger movement provides self-imposed doctrinal constraints for the individual congregations.

Both congregational and presbyterian polities normally reject the term "priest": ordained leaders are referred to as "pastors" or "ministers".

While it is the local church that ordains ministers in a congregational model, the larger movement will have a process for accrediting the ordained ministers across the movement. This is convenient for satisfying official government requirements for ministers of religion. It also facilitates the movement of pastors from one congregation to another.

As a measure of the differences between these three models, consider who has the authority to license a minister or to stand a minister down from their pastoral office. In episcopal polity, it is the bishop of the diocese. In presbyterian polity, it is the presbytery or the assembly. In congregational polity, it is the local elders or the members themselves. These three scenarios point clearly to where authority lies.

These differing polities generate different church cultures. An Anglican pastor is accountable for their teaching to their bishop. A Presbyterian pastor is accountable to the presbytery and the assembly. A Baptist pastor is accountable to the members of their congregation: one sermon received badly could result in a Baptist pastor being removed from their position by a vote of the members.

MIXED MODELS

Some denominations have a mixture of different kinds of polity. For example, even though the Baptist model is basically congregational, in Victoria it is the Baptist Union of Victoria that ordains people to ministry, not local congregations, while in New South Wales, Baptist congregations conduct ordinations but the state body accredits ministers beyond the local congregation, for example, to register them with the government as marriage celebrants. As another example of a mixed polity, although bishops in the Anglican tradition are the fundamental source of authority for ministry, and church polity is episcopal, Anglican dioceses in Australia also have synods, which are assemblies comprising clergy and lay people who meet in conjunction with, and led by, their bishop as the "bishop-in-synod". There is also a national Anglican General Synod, chaired by the Anglican Primate, who is appointed for a six-year term. The Primate's role at General Synod is akin to that of a Moderator in the Presbyterian system: the Anglican Primate is elected, serves for a fixed term, and does not exercise direct executive authority over the dioceses or their bishops. The Primate has such authority only in their own diocese.

WHO SPEAKS FOR "THE RELIGION"?

Denominations, movements, and many individual congregations normally have a set of constituting theological and ethical statements to which members and ministers must adhere. These provide guidance about and set limits on the doctrine of the group. Many Christian churches include the

> Churches normally have constituting statements to which their members must adhere.

Nicene Creed, the *Apostles' Creed* and the *Athanasian Creed* among their defining documents. In addition, several longer-established Protestant traditions have historical documents that they rely on, such as the *Belgic Confession* (1561), the *Heidelberg Catechism* (1563), the *Thirty-nine Articles* (1571), the *Canons of Dort* (1619) and the *Westminster Confession of Faith* (1646).

References to the authority of the Bible form an important part of these documents, establishing the Bible as the primary constituting doctrinal document. The Anglican tradition also looks to officially recognised prayer books and the *Ordinal* (the rite for making priests, bishops, and deacons) alongside its *Thirty-nine Articles*.

> For most churches, the Bible is the primary constituting doctrinal document.

Many congregations and multi-congregational movements have drafted their own doctrinal statements. For example, the Vineyard Churches of Australia, an evangelical movement which came to Australia in 1995 and now comprises 16 congregations, has adopted a *Statement of Faith* which lays out 15 core beliefs in around 1,000 words.[29]

Some denominations have a much more detailed summary statement of their teaching and expectations of adherents. An example is the *Catechism of the Catholic Church* (1992), a book of 848 pages of fine print. The catechism of the Anglican Church in North America, *To Be a Christian: An Anglican Catechism* (2020), does the job in 160 pages. On the other hand, some denominations or movements have quite pithy doctrinal statements, leaving it up to the local congregation or pastor to flesh out the details.

---

29 vineyard.org.au/statement-of-faith

An example is the Australian branch of the anti-clerical Exclusive Brethren movement, which holds to the Bible as its sole and supreme authority in regard to doctrine and expects each local congregation to know how to put that principle into practice. In interpreting and applying the Bible, the Exclusive Brethren are constrained by a tradition, passed on through their communities, rather than by catechisms or constitutions.[30] It is indeed a matter of pride that the denomination's doctrine is solely based on the Bible.

This arrangement, which relies heavily on shared communal memory, created a vulnerability for the Exclusive Brethren in 2010 when they faced an anti-discrimination complaint in Victoria.

> The Brethren's lack of a formal constituting doctrinal statement has made them legally vulnerable.

In the absence of a formal doctrinal statement, how was a secular tribunal to determine what the Exclusive Brethren "religion" should be deemed to be, and what its doctrines were? This was a legal disability which the Catholic Church would not have suffered, because its doctrines are laid out in great detail in its *Catechism*.

The failure of the Exclusive Brethren to convince a secular tribunal that their sincerely held views on human sexuality were part of their religious doctrines has served as a lesson for other churches, some of whom have moved to include a protective clause about marriage in their doctrinal statements. An example is the brief 246-word doctrinal statement of Acts Global Churches, a

---

30 The teachings of John Nelson Darby (d. 1882) have been important in shaping that tradition.

Pentecostal denomination, which now includes a statement that marriage is a "union of a man and a woman".[31]

DISCIPLINE

Just as Christian denominations and movements vary in where they locate authority and in how detailed their doctrinal prescriptions are, they also vary in their appetite for demanding conformity with their requirements, including assent to their official doctrines. Church discipline has legal implications in Australia, since anti-discrimination laws speak of whether conduct "conforms" with the "doctrines of the religion". The idea of "conforms" assumes the application of church discipline.

Suppose a denomination has a requirement written into their code of conduct for ministers that they should practise chastity if single and sexual faithfulness in marriage. Suppose, furthermore, that a minister in the denomination is found to be having an affair. Standing that minister down from their position would be an act of church discipline—of requiring that the minister conform to the requirements of the religion.

Church discipline cannot be reduced to secular ethical norms, so in order to accommodate doctrinal requirements, religions are granted certain exemptions to anti-discrimination laws. In Australia, it would be discriminatory and illegal for a secular company to sack an employee for practising

> Church discipline cannot be reduced to secular ethical norms.

---

31 actsglobal.church/Public/About_Us/Public/About_Us/What_we_believe.aspx

Hinduism, but a Christian minister who was found to be practising Hinduism would lose their job—in most denominations, if not all!

Most churches consider discipline to be important as it safeguards the doctrine and ethics of a church. However, churches vary greatly in how willing they are to apply it. Some denominations are liberal in accommodating divergence from stated requirements; others have requirements that are difficult to enforce because they are vague; others can be selective in which requirements they insist on and which they are willing to overlook; and still others have a high expectation of compliance.

> Not all churches have the same appetite for doctrinal conformity.

An example of denominational tolerance in North America was Bishop Shelby Spong's continuation in office as the Episcopal Bishop of Newark, New Jersey after publicly declaring that he had rejected core Christian beliefs, including the deity of Christ, the virgin birth, and the resurrection. It may seem incongruous that a bishop, as part of regular worship, could lead a congregation in reciting creeds articulating doctrines yet profess to disbelieve those very same doctrines—even having sworn an oath, as part of his induction to the office of bishop, to guard the faith of the church, a faith which is summarised in those creeds.

Denominations can vary internally in their approach to discipline, with some branches of a denomination stricter in applying discipline than others. Diocesan bishops within the same denomination may be more or less tolerant in the way they manage dissenting voices or non-conforming conduct among the clergy. In one Anglican diocese, having an affair could lead to cancellation of a minister's licence and loss of all prospects of re-employment. In another diocese, the same breach of the same code of conduct might result in little more than a pastoral conversation with the bishop or, at most, a move to another appointment.

> Church discipline should be applied consistently across a denomination.

Ideally, discipline should be applied consistently across a denomination. To do otherwise could be considered unfair. However, in churches with multiple centres of authority—for example, the Anglican Church of Australia—it seems inevitable that discipline will be applied inconsistently from one diocese to another.

One can distinguish between hard discipline and soft discipline. Hard discipline is the capacity and willingness of church authorities to remove a leader from office if they do not conform to the church's doctrinal or ethical requirements. Soft discipline is exercised through gate-keeping power when making appointments, by filtering out people who do not or are unlikely to meet the requirements, and by counselling and putting other forms of pressure on those who already occupy positions. It is rare for the Catholic Church to exercise hard discipline to sack a diocesan bishop. However, it is just business as usual for a pope to be selective in whom they will consecrate to the office of bishop. In this way, soft discipline can shape the doctrinal trajectory of the whole Catholic Church.

In the history of Protestant denominations, breakaway groups have often formed when some members have felt that their denomination has become too lax, wandering away from core principles and neglecting to impose discipline.

For example, in 2003, North American Episcopalians ignored the Lambeth Resolution 1.10 (1998) on human sexuality when they appointed Gene Robinson, an openly partnered gay man, as Bishop of New Hampshire. Although Lambeth resolutions are not binding upon the global Anglican church, the Global Anglican Future Conference movement, which was launched in 2008, was a reaction against the refusal of the Archbishop of Canterbury to disinvite from the Lambeth conference those North American Anglican bishops who supported Robinson's election. It was for this same reason that a meeting of the GAFCON movement in early 2023 rejected the leadership of the Archbishop of Canterbury in the global Anglican Communion. (It was reported at the time that the GAFCON movement's leaders represented 85% of the world's Anglicans.)

4

DENOMINATIONS AND MOVEMENTS

The history of Christianity is complex. Here is a simple summary overview of the branching of Christian denominations, and the resulting denominations and movements in Australia.

THE GLOBAL HISTORY OF CHRISTIANITY

Divisions in Christianity go back to the time of the first followers of Jesus. There are references to conflicting teachings and sectarian divisions in the New Testament. Major divisions continued to develop in the first centuries on doctrinal and geopolitical grounds. Later, the Protestant Reformation resulted in a separate major branch developing, and the Pentecostal movement in the 20th century created another offshoot. There are the following high-level

> Divisions in Christianity go back to the time of the first followers of Jesus.

traditions of Christianity, based on shared characteristics, all of which are represented in Australia:

1. Nestorian Churches (separated AD 431 over a Christological[32] controversy). Examples: Mar Thoma Church of India, Assyrian Church of the East. Polity: episcopal.

2. Oriental Orthodox Churches (separated AD 451 over a Christological controversy). Examples: Coptic Church of Egypt, Ethiopian Orthodox Church, Syrian Orthodox Church, Eritrean Orthodox Church. Polity: episcopal.

3. Eastern Orthodox Churches (separated from the Western Church in 1054 as a result of accumulated differences). Examples: Greek Orthodox Church, Russian Orthodox Church, Serbian Orthodox Church, Romanian Orthodox Church. Polity: episcopal.

4. Western Churches (further split in two by the Protestant Reformation in the 16th century):

    4.1. The Roman Catholic Church. Polity: episcopal.

    4.2. Protestant churches, consisting of:

    a. National State Churches and denominations derived from state churches. Examples: Lutheran Churches, Church of England and Anglican denominations. Polity: episcopal and presbyterian.

    b. Non-conformist or "free" churches established by reform movements in reaction against state churches. Examples: Baptists, Church

---

32 Christology is a branch of theology that concerns the nature of Christ as both human and divine.

of Christ, Presbyterians. Polity: presbyterian and congregational.

c. Pentecostal and Charismatic churches. Examples: CRC Churches International, Australian Christian Churches (ACC), Acts Global Churches, Vineyard Churches of Australia. Polity: various, but normally congregational.

d. Diverse global Christian movements, most of which arose during the 20th century. Examples: indigenous African movements, independent Chinese house churches. Polity: various.

The Western (European) church was divided by the Protestant Reformation. This produced multiple movements that rejected the authority of the Roman Pope and sought to reform Christianity by restoring it to the teachings of the Bible. These movements can be divided into state churches and non-conformist (or "free") churches. Early Protestant Reformation movements included Anabaptists, Calvinism (shaped by the teachings of John Calvin in Geneva), and Lutheranism (shaped by the teachings of Martin Luther in Germany).

> Protestant churches can be divided into state churches and non-conformist churches.

The term *Reformed* is used of Protestant churches and theology in the Calvinist tradition. European nations where Reformed churches became well established include Scotland (the Presbyterians), the Netherlands, and, for a time, France, until the St Bartholomew's Day massacre of the Huguenots in

1572. From these roots, Reformed Christianity spread to North America, Africa, Indonesia, Korea, and many other countries.

The English Reformation was significantly shaped by Calvinism and the Reformed tradition: the Royal Coronation Oath has the sovereign swear allegiance to the "Protestant Reformed Religion established by law".

Throughout the 18th and 19th centuries, evangelical revivals (also known as "awakenings") in the UK and the USA resulted in the formation of new movements and denominations, which in turn gave rise to other movements. For example, the Salvation Army was an offshoot of Methodism, which was an offshoot of the Church of England.

Pentecostal movements, starting from Los Angeles at the turn of the 20th century, developed out of earlier evangelical Protestant movements. Their membership now numbers in the hundreds of millions.

> Pentecostals now number in the hundreds of millions.

There is also a large number of contemporary indigenous Christian movements around the world that do not easily fit within the above categories, including underground Chinese Christian house churches and many African movements which grew out of foundations laid by Western Protestant missions, some of which have sent missionaries to plant congregations in Australia. These new movements are mostly evangelical and/or Pentecostal in character. Their governance is diverse.

These worldwide Pentecostal and indigenous Christian movements have much in common with the Protestant tradition, but it makes little sense to call them "Western", even though they may trace historical roots to European Protestant missions.

Protestant denominations make up around 40% of the global Christian population and the majority of these are Pentecostals or Charismatics.[33] Roman Catholics make up around half of the global total.

Although all these branches of Christianity have an active presence in Australia, when people speak of "Christians" or "Christianity" in Australia, they tend to think of the dominant Catholic and Protestant offshoots of the Western branch, and many still mistakenly think of Christianity as a Western religion. Nevertheless, Australia has lively, growing communities of the ancient Eastern branches of Christianity, as well as missionary congregations planted by indigenous Christian movements sent here from other nations including Nigeria and Brazil. These are a reminder that Christianity in Australia is not a Western religion, and not necessarily associated with a European cultural heritage.

> Many mistakenly think of Christianity as a Western religion.

Some branches of Christianity are in obvious decline in Western nations, with many church buildings standing empty, or being deconsecrated, sold off, and redeveloped. At the same time, over the past century, global Christianity has been going through a period of vibrant expansion. For example, Pentecostal and Charismatic churches, having developed out of a movement that began just over a century ago, today number

> Global Christianity has been going through a period of vibrant expansion.

---

33 pewresearch.org/religion/2011/12/19/global-christianity-movements-and-denominations

hundreds of millions of worshippers. These global trends have also impacted churches in Australia. For example, the second-largest movement of Christians in Australia, measured in terms of weekly attendance, is the Pentecostals. This movement did not exist in Australia 120 years ago.

DENOMINATIONS IN AUSTRALIA

There are three important sources of information about the state of Christianity in Australia. These are the National Census, conducted by the Australian Bureau of Statistics; the Australian National Church Life Survey (NCLS), which assesses patterns of attendance and church health across the country; and data gathered by individual denominations.

The Australian Census of 2021 offered the following options to those who consider themselves to be adherents of a Christian "religion":

- Catholic
- Anglican (Church of England)
- Uniting Church
- Presbyterian
- Greek Orthodox
- Baptist
- Other (the respondent had to specify)

The Bureau of Statistics reported the following results from the 2021 Census for "Christian" affiliation, comprising 43.8% of the Australia's population (Table 1).

DENOMINATIONS AND MOVEMENTS

	2021 Census	Change since 2016 Census
Anglican	2,496,273	-24.2%
Baptist	347,334	0.6%
Brethren	18,258	4.6%
Catholic	5,075,907	-4.3%
Churches of Christ	35,928	-10.3%
Jehovah's Witnesses	84,405	2.2%
Mormons	57,868	-6.5%
Lutheran	145,868	-19.3%
Oriental Orthodox	60,774	16.1%
Assyrian Apostolic	19,141	27.6%
Eastern Orthodox	535,470	6.1%
Presbyterian & Reformed	414,882	-26.9%
Salvation Army	35,356	-38.4%
Seventh-day Adventist	63,662	1.1%
Uniting Church	673,260	-29.2%
Pentecostal	255,838	-1.8%
Other Protestant	112,474	3.7%
Other Christian	27,679	-10.4%
Christianity, not further defined	688,440	11.0%
Total	11,148,814	-9.4%

Table 1. Christian affiliation in the 2021 Census

In 2011, 6% of respondents just wrote "Christian" or "Christianity" on their Census form, and this has been the fastest growing Census category of Christians over the past 30 years. Although the question asks for people's "religion" in terms of denominations, many Australian Christians, if asked to identify their religion outside of a Census data collection exercise, would just call themselves "Christian" rather than use a denominational label. Denominations are a less significant part of Australian Christians' identity than they used to be.

I have been made very conscious of the weakening of denominational identities, especially among Protestants, during recent years through teaching theology. At the beginning of each course, I invite students to share their denominational history.

> Denominational labels no longer have much significance for many Australian Christians.

With a few exceptions, it is almost always diverse. One student grew up in a Pentecostal church, then joined a Reformed church, and later became a Latin Mass Catholic. Another grew up in an Anglican church, then, after marrying, moved to his wife's Church of Christ congregation. After some time, their Bible study group morphed into a non-denominational church which now identifies with the Baptist tradition. Another grew up in a Malay Chinese Pentecostal church, then moved to a Presbyterian church. Another grew up in a Pentecostal church, then later she joined a Baptist church. After moving to the outback, she was attending a Baptist church as well as a non-denominational Aboriginal church. Now she attends a Baptist seminary and an Anglican congregation on Sundays. Another grew up in an Australian Romanian Baptist church and now attends a non-denominational church. Another became a Christian while living with his mother in a haunted house in Melbourne. When Christian pastors cleansed their home of spirits, he and his mother became Christians. For a time, he served as a pastor in a Pentecostal church that has its headquarters in Taiwan, and now he leads a Chinese congregation in an Anglican church. Another was a Hindu Brahmin priest for many years, became a Christian while in medical school, and now attends a very conservative Brethren church.

Australian churches are full of people like these whose religious identity is simply Christian. Their denominational identity is weaker or non-existent because it is transitory and, in their understanding, changeable.

The Census questions on religion hark back to another era, when individuals and families had stable, life-long religious denominational identities such as "Anglican", "Catholic", "Presbyterian", "Methodist", or "Baptist". Today the Census questions are out-dated.

> The Census questions on religion are outdated.

The most striking anomaly about the Census is that although there are more Australian Pentecostals than Anglicans in Australian churches on Sundays, "Pentecostal" does not rate a mention in the Census question. The conservatism of the Census is also reflected in the inclusion of the phrase "Church of England", despite the fact that there has been no actual "Church of England" in Australia since the name of the denomination was changed to "Anglican Church of Australia" more than forty years ago. Hardly anyone who attends an Anglican Church uses the "Church of England" label anymore.

Media commentary on Australian religions often refers to Census box tickers as "members". From this perspective, in 2021 the Australian Anglican Church had over two million "members". This is fanciful: it is not at all how most denominations and religious movements function. These Census figures reflect social labels that people accept, not their actual participation in churches or even their personal faith. A more meaningful measure of denominational health is the number of those actually involved enough to worship week by week; in comparison, the National Census data are very misleading.

Denomination	%
Catholic	11%
Pentecostal	>100%
Anglican	5%
Baptist	33%
Uniting	10%

Table 2. Weekly worship attendance as a percentage of Australian Census figures[34]

The extent of nominalism varies greatly from denomination to denomination. NCLS Research (using National Church Life Survey data) has published estimates of weekly attendance as a percentage of Census figures (Table 1). Their research shows that one in three declared Baptists is in church on any given Sunday, but only one in 20 declared Anglicans darkens their local church's door. There are more people attending Pentecostal churches each week than write "Pentecostal" on their Census forms!

> Census figures reflect social labels, not personal faith or participation in a church.

Despite their usefulness, even average weekly attendance figures are not a direct reflection of the numbers of actively practising worshippers. This is because in many churches, for every 100

---

34 Ruth Powell, Sam Sterland, and Miriam Pepper. 2020. *The Resilient Church: Affiliation, Attendance and Size in Australia.* NCLS Occasional Paper 43. Sydney: NCLS Research.

average attenders in church on a Sunday, there could be another 50 to 100 people who attend that church often enough to be considered active participants in the congregation, but are not there every single week.

> Pentecostals are now the second-largest Christian group.

What the Australian Census data conceal is the fact that for at least the past decade, Pentecostals have been the second-largest Australian Christian group, in terms of attendance, after Catholics and ahead of Anglicans. In 2016, in terms of attendance, the top five churches in order of size were:

Denomination	%
Catholic	39%
Australian Christian Churches	12%
Anglican	10%
Baptist	7%
Uniting	6%

Table 3. The five largest Christian denominations in Australia, by share of weekly attendances[35]

Note that only the largest Pentecostal denomination, Australian Christian Churches, is reported here. The overall Pentecostal share of weekly worshippers will be still greater.

Other important differences between denominations are that they vary greatly in their age profiles and in their growth/decline trends. NCLS researchers Ruth Powell and Sam Sterland have

---

35 Ruth Powell. 2019. *Church Vitality: NCLS Leaders Briefing.* Sydney: NCLS Research. By 2011, ACC was only slightly under the Anglicans, and it is only one of several growing Pentecostal movements.

surveyed these trends and group the Western church tradition into four categories:[36]

- Catholic
- Mainstream Protestant (including Anglican, Lutheran, Presbyterian, Uniting)
- Other Protestant (including Baptist, Churches of Christ, Seventh-day Adventist, Salvation Army, Christian Reformed Churches of Australia, Christian Missionary Alliance, Wesleyan Methodist, Vineyard Fellowship Australia, Church of the Nazarene)
- Pentecostal (including Australian Christian Churches, International Network of Churches, Global Acts Churches, C3 Church Global, CRC Churches International).

The story of Australian Christianity has not been one of uniform decline. While the "Catholic" and "Mainstream Protestant" churches have been declining, the "Other Protestant" and "Pentecostal" churches have been growing, and the net effect of these trends is an increase in overall Protestant church attendance despite mainstream Protestant decline.[37]

> The story of Australian Christianity is not one of uniform decline.

One of the important features of church growth and decline across Australia is that recent immigrants from Asia,

---

36 Ruth Powell and Sam Sterland. 2019. *Community and Church Summit and NCLS Leaders Briefing Summary.* Ruth Powell. 2019. *Church Vitality.*

37 Ruth Powell, Sam Sterland, and Miriam Pepper. 2020. *The Resilient Church.*

Africa, and the Pacific prefer to attend growing churches with a younger demographic. This matches the trajectory of global Christianity: white Christianity may be in decline but non-white Christianity is growing vibrantly.

> White Christianity may be in decline, but non-white Christianity is growing vibrantly.

While some denominations are ageing, which correlates with declining attendance, the growing "Other Protestant" and "Pentecostal" categories have higher participation of younger members than the declining "Catholic" and "Mainstream Protestant" denominations. The Uniting Church's top four age cohorts in the 2016 National Census comprised people aged 50–69, while Pentecostal churches' top four adult age cohorts comprised 15–34-year-olds. Likewise, 2016 NCLS data on weekly attendance revealed that around one-quarter of attenders in Pentecostal churches were aged between 15 and 29, but in the Uniting Church, two-thirds (67%) of attenders were aged 60 or older.[38]

In light of these Uniting Church figures, it is noteworthy that in the 2016 Census, only 44% of Uniting Church adult respondents were aged 60 or more. This discrepancy in attendance patterns reflects the fact that Uniting Church nominalism is greater among the young. This is another way in which Census statistics misrepresent the health of Australian churches: they can give the impression that an ageing denomination has a younger profile than it actually has.

---

38 Ruth Powell, Miriam Pepper, Kathy Jacka, and Sam Sterland. 2018. *Vista: Scanning the Landscape of Local Churches in Australia.* Sydney: NCLS Research.

As a rule, the faster growing churches also set a higher bar in terms of their doctrinal conservatism. In Australia, the Uniting Church is the most theologically liberal and progressive denomination, and is also one of the most rapidly declining and the fastest ageing. This pattern is being repeated in Western nations around the world. As Duane Miller put it in his survey of the last 60 years of global Anglicanism, "Demographic trends point to the eventual extinction of the progressive Anglican wing."[39] The link between progressivism and denominational decline exists in other mainstream denominations as well.

> "Trends point to the eventual extinction of the progressive Anglican wing."
> – Duane Miller

In the following chapters we will consider the position of five different church traditions—all branches of Western Christianity—on the issue of human sexuality and, in particular, same-sex marriage.[40] We will see that the Catholic Church in Australia is holding to a conservative doctrinal position despite having a progressively inclined membership; the Australian Anglican Church is in conflict over this issue and is engaged in a long drawn-out process of dividing; the Uniting Church is affirming same-sex attraction, but not without significant dissent from some congregations and ministers; the Presbyterian Church and the small, conservative Free Reformed Church of Australia, like the Catholic Church, both hold to a conservative position; and Pentecostal churches are holding to a conservative position.

---

39 Duane A. Miller. 2023. "Mission and disintegration in global Anglicanism from the 1960s through 2022: an update to Stephen Neill's *Anglicanism.*" *Global Missiology* 20(1):64–71.

40 While the ancient Eastern churches are not considered here, they are all conservative in doctrine and ethics.

5

THE CATHOLIC CHURCH

In the Catholic Church, sometimes referred to as the Roman Catholic Church, doctrine is articulated to a high degree of detail. The totality of Catholic doctrine is brought together in summary form in the *Catechism of the Catholic Church*, an official compendium of Catholic teachings. This catechism was promulgated by Pope John Paul II by means of the Apostolic Constitution, *Fide Depositum*, in 1992.

The doctrines laid out in the Catholic *Catechism* are derived from God's revelation of himself through the Bible as well as through the "Apostolic Tradition", which is the teaching of Jesus passed on orally by the apostles. Furthermore,

> Catholic doctrine is brought together in the *Catechism of the Catholic Church*.

the Catechism explains that God's self-communication "remains present and active in the Church" (§79): there can be a process of development of doctrine. The *Catechism* therefore cites many thousands of Bible verses, together with references to the teachers of the Church from the past, as authorities for its teachings.

The Bishop of Rome, known as the Pope, is not infallible in himself, but certain statements by him, issued under specific circumstances, are considered to be doctrinally binding for the Church. This occurs when the Pope speaks *ex cathedra* (from the chair of St Peter) on issues of faith and ethics. It is rare for popes to do this.

The Pope has the final say in the appointment of bishops and cardinals and, in practice, this is more important in its power to influence the church than his ability to speak *ex cathedra*. It is the cardinals aged under 80 who elect the Pope; bishops are the ones who decide who are ordained as priests; and the priests are the ones who do most of the teaching of lay people.

> The Pope has the final say in the appointment of bishops and cardinals.

The *Catechism of the Catholic Church*[41] treats ethics mainly under its exposition of the Ten Commandments, and the issue of sexual purity is covered under the heading of the sixth[42] commandment, "You shall not commit adultery". The *Catechism* states, "The tradition of the Church has understood the sixth commandment as encompassing the whole of human sexuality" (§2336).[43]

---

41 www.vatican.va/archive/ENG0015/_INDEX.HTM

42 There are variations in how the Ten Commandments are counted: while Protestants generally consider the prohibition of adultery to be the seventh commandment, the Catholic Church counts it as the sixth.

43 The relevant passages are found in Part 3 of the *Catechism*, entitled "Life in Christ". Section 2 of Part 3 is devoted to the Ten Commandments.

Key points of the Catholic position on homosexuality, as articulated in the *Catechism*, are:

- God created human beings male and female and blessed their union. (§2331)
- The complementarity of man and woman is "oriented" towards marriage and family life. (§2333)
- The union of a man and woman in marriage "is a way of imitating in the flesh the Creator's generosity and fecundity: 'Therefore a man leaves his father and his mother and cleaves to his wife, and they become one flesh' [Genesis 2:24]." (§2335)
- "Lust is disordered desire for or inordinate enjoyment of sexual pleasure. Sexual pleasure is morally disordered when sought for itself, isolated from its procreative and unitive[44] purposes." (§2351)

> "Sexual pleasure is morally disordered when sought for itself."
> – Catholic *Catechism*

- "Basing itself on Sacred Scripture, which presents homosexual acts as acts of grave depravity, tradition has always declared that 'homosexual acts are intrinsically disordered.'[45] They are contrary to the natural law. They close the sexual act to the gift of life. They do not proceed from a genuine affective and sexual complementarity.

---

44   The word *unitive* here refers to heterosexual union.
45   The *Catechism* takes this quotation from *Persona Humana* §8, published by the Sacred Congregation for the Doctrine of the Faith in 1975. www.vatican.va/roman_curia/congregations/cfaith/documents/rc_con_cfaith_doc_19751229_persona-humana_en.html

Under no circumstances can they be approved." (§2357) This paragraph references the following Bible passages:

- Genesis 19:1–29. The account of the destruction of Sodom and Gomorrah.

- Romans 1:24–27: "Therefore God gave them over in the sinful desires of their hearts to sexual impurity for the degrading of their bodies with one another. They exchanged the truth about God for a lie, and worshiped and served created things rather than the Creator—who is forever praised. Amen.

  Because of this, God gave them over to shameful lusts. Even their women exchanged natural sexual relations for unnatural ones. In the same way the men also abandoned natural relations with women and were inflamed with lust for one another. Men committed shameful acts with other men, and received in themselves the due penalty for their error."

- 1 Corinthians 6:9: "Or do you not know that wrongdoers will not inherit the kingdom of God? Do not be deceived: Neither the sexually immoral nor idolaters nor adulterers nor men who have sex with men."

- 1 Timothy 1:9–10: "We also know that the law is made not for the righteous but for lawbreakers and rebels, the ungodly and sinful, the unholy and irreligious, for those who kill their fathers or mothers, for murderers, for the sexually immoral, for those practicing homosexuality, for slave traders and liars and perjurers—and for whatever else is contrary to the sound doctrine."

- "The number of men and women who have deep-seated homosexual tendencies is not negligible. This inclination, which is objectively disordered, constitutes for most of them a trial. They must be accepted with respect, compassion, and sensitivity. Every sign of unjust discrimination in their regard should be avoided. These persons are called to fulfil God's will in their lives and, if they are Christians, to unite to the sacrifice of the Lord's Cross the difficulties they may encounter from their condition." (§2358)

- "Homosexual persons are called to chastity. By the virtues of self-mastery that teach them inner freedom, at times by the support of disinterested friendship, by prayer and sacramental grace, they can and should gradually and resolutely approach Christian perfection." (§2359)

- "The sexual act must take place exclusively within marriage. Outside of marriage it always constitutes a grave sin and excludes one from sacramental communion." (§2390)

- [In a summary section]: "Among the sins gravely contrary to chastity are masturbation, fornication, pornography, and homosexual practices." (§2396)

Clearly, the settled doctrine of the Catholic Church is that homosexual acts are sinful. Pope Francis has repeatedly commended Catholics to love all people, whatever their sexual orientation, but such statements do not reflect or intimate a change in doctrine. Rather, the current Pope

> The settled doctrine of the Catholic Church is that homosexual acts are sinful.

has repeatedly affirmed official Catholic teachings on marriage and homosexuality.

Of course, there are many Catholics who disagree with their Church's teachings on sexuality, but in a very real sense it is not open to them to hold contrary views, as is shown by the *Catechism*, whose purpose is to define what is to be taught to Catholic believers and what they are to believe. Any Catholic believer who believed and acted consistently with the teachings contained in the *Catechism of the Catholic Church* would be adhering to the settled doctrine of the religion of the Catholic Church. To the extent that someone holds views that diverge from the *Catechism*, they are following their own religion, not that of the Catholic Church.

DISCIPLINE AND COMPLIANCE

There can be a gap between the teachings of the Catholic Church and what ordinary Catholics believe and do, and the scandals of sexual abuse of children have weakened the Catholic Church's moral authority to regulate the sexual ethics of its members. The Catholic Church has sometimes acted in ways that enabled infringements of sexual ethics by clergy, most infamously in the abuse of children. (This is true of other Christian denominations as well.) This has been changing as the influence of public scrutiny has brought greater accountability. In the past, it used to be quite difficult for Catholic bishops to dismiss clergy, due to the demanding nature of a formal

> Sexual abuse of children has weakened the Catholic Church's moral authority.

canon law trial, but in 2009, Pope Benedict gave increased powers to bishops to defrock priests for sexual misconduct.[46]

What is not likely to change is Rome's ethical policies relating to same-sex activity involving consenting adults. This is not to say that there are no moves for change. In March 2023, an assembly of German bishops and lay people voted to introduce a blessing for German same-sex couples. Out of an assembly of 202, 176 approved the change, only 14 voted against, and 12 abstained.[47] The German Catholic Church is known to be one of the most, if not the most liberal in the world: the *International Survey of Catholic Women* found that German women reported the highest level of support for same-sex marriage of all the countries surveyed.[48] (Australian Catholic women were evenly divided on this issue, with 33% strongly in favour, and 33% strongly against.)

The 2023 Synod on Synodality in Rome brought forward some of the German bishops' proposals for the blessing of same-sex unions. Nevertheless, this initiative, even if embraced in Germany, will not meet with Rome's approval

---

46 theguardian.com/world/2009/jun/08/catholic-bishops-powers-dismiss-priests

47 ncronline.org/news/germanys-catholic-bishops-vote-approve-blessings-same-sex-couples

48 Tracy McEwan, Kathleen McPhillips and Miriam Pepper. 2023. *International Survey of Catholic Women: Analysis and Report of Findings*. University of Newcastle, p.52. In this survey, the two other Catholic countries which approached Germany in their liberalism were Spain and Ireland.

6

THE ANGLICAN CHURCH

Around the world, churches referred to as "Anglican" have developed out of the Church of England. In 1981, the "Church of England in Australia" changed its name to the "Anglican Church of Australia".

The positions of Australian Anglicans on same-sex relations are complex and conflicted. While all sides would affirm that same-sex attracted people should be treated with love and compassion, Anglicans disagree on whether homosexual acts are sinful and thus a breach of sexual purity and holiness. They consequently also differ on whether same-sex attracted people should be able to have their relationships blessed by the Church and be married in the sight of God. These differences among Australian Anglicans are widely known and have been repeatedly commented on in the media.

> The positions of Australian Anglicans on same-sex relations are complex and conflicted.

To understand the situation that applies in the Anglican Church of Australia, it needs to be understood that the Roman Catholic Church's capacity to issue detailed authoritative declarations of doctrine and ethics is not shared by the Anglican Church. The doctrinal foundations of Protestant denominations are less articulated with less detailed guidance on ethics: there is nothing comparable to the *Catechism of the Catholic Church* to which all Anglicans are expected to adhere.

> There is nothing like the Catholic *Catechism* to which all Anglicans should adhere.

The Anglican approach to setting doctrinal standards is to determine a set of core beliefs, which are written down and must be adhered to. The rest is left to pastors and congregations to determine, in accordance with fundamental principles, under the oversight of their bishops.

Anglican tradition has historically built a doctrinal basis on the Bible, the *Thirty-Nine Articles of Religion of the Church of England*, the *Church of England Prayer Book* of 1662 (revised in 1928), and the *Ordinal* (the rite for the making of deacons, priests, and bishops).

Concerning the Bible, Article VI of the *Thirty-nine Articles* states that:

> "Holy Scripture containeth all things necessary to salvation: so that whatsoever is not read therein, or may be proved thereby, is not to be required of any man, that it should be believed as an article of the Faith, or be thought requisite or necessary to salvation."

This principle limits Anglican clergy to teach as "necessary to salvation" only what can be demonstrated from the Bible (the Old and New Testaments, without the Apocryphal books). In contrast to the Catholic Church's *Catechism*, the *Thirty-nine Articles* do not include any specific teachings about adultery or sexual activity in general, but have only an affirmation of "obedience" to the "Commandments which are called Moral" (Article VII), a formulation which includes the Ten Commandments.

Although it was not formalised in Anglicanism's constituting documents, the traditional Anglican view of homosexuality is similar to that of the Catholic Church, being grounded in the same Bible passages. However, in recent years, some Anglicans have revised this understanding.

GRADUAL DISENGAGEMENT

Every ten years, bishops of churches in communion with the Church of England meet at Lambeth in England at the invitation of the Archbishop of Canterbury. The 1998 Lambeth gathering adopted Resolution I.10 on human sexuality, which incorporated a Subsection Report worded as follows:

> "We must confess that we are not of one mind about homosexuality."
> – Anglican bishops

> We must confess that we are not of one mind about homosexuality. Our variety of understanding encompasses:
>
> - those who believe that homosexuality is a disorder, but that through the grace of Christ people can be changed, although not without pain and struggle.

- those who believe that relationships between people of the same gender should not include genital expression, that this is the clear teaching of the Bible and of the Church universal, and that such activity (if unrepented of) is a barrier to the Kingdom of God.

- those who believe that committed homosexual relationships fall short of the biblical norm, but are to be preferred to relationships that are anonymous and transient.

- those who believe that the Church should accept and support or bless monogamous covenant relationships between homosexual people and that they may be ordained.

Nevertheless, Resolution I.10 affirmed that:

The Holy Scriptures and Christian tradition teach that human sexuality is intended by God to find its rightful and full expression between a man and a woman in the covenant of marriage, established by God in creation and affirmed by our Lord Jesus Christ. Holy Matrimony is, by intention and divine purpose, to be a life-long monogamous and unconditional commitment between a woman and a man.

It also reported that "clearly the opinion of the majority of bishops is not prepared to bless same-sex unions or to ordain active homosexuals". However, "we have prayed, studied and discussed these issues, and we are unable to reach a common mind on the scriptural, theological, historical, and scientific questions which are raised".

Resolution I.10, adopted by the gathering of bishops, specifically rejected "homosexual practice as incompatible with Scripture", but called upon Anglicans to "minister pastorally to all irrespective of sexual orientation, and to condemn irrational fear of homosexuals, violence within marriage and any trivialisation and commercialisation of sex". This resolution reflected the majority view of Anglican bishops at the time, but Lambeth resolutions are not legally binding upon Anglican diocese.

> The Lambeth conference called upon Anglicans to "minister pastorally to all irrespective of sexual orientation".

Since 1998, many developments around this issue have taken place, including divisions in national Anglican churches.[49] Some examples are:

- Bishops from Rwanda and Southeast Asia intervened in the United States to consecrate missionary bishops for the United States in 2000, effectively establishing an Anglican Church in the USA that was distinct from the Episcopal Church in the USA (ECUSA) and retained a traditional Christian understanding of human sexuality. This movement came to be known as the Anglican Mission in the Americas.

- In 2003, openly partnered gay priest Gene Robinson was consecrated Bishop of New Hampshire by ECUSA bishops.

- The then Archbishop of Canterbury, Rowan Williams, invited the North American bishops involved in Gene Robinson's consecration to the 2008 Lambeth meeting. Many bishops were disappointed that the Archbishop of

---

49 For an overview of developments, see Duane A. Miller. 2023. "Mission and disintegration in global Anglicanism."

Canterbury seemed unwilling to discipline the ECUSA bishops by disinviting them, even though they had acted against Resolution I.10 in consecrating Gene Robinson. In protest at the consecration of Gene Robinson, around 230 Anglican bishops boycotted the Lambeth conference.

- An alternative meeting, the Global Anglican Future Conference, was held in Jerusalem and attended by many of the bishops who had absented themselves from Lambeth. This conference launched the GAFCON movement, which has emerged as a global Anglican alignment in competition with and in rejection of Lambeth and the Archbishop of Canterbury's leadership.

> GAFCON has emerged as a global Anglican alignment that rejects the Archbishop of Canterbury's leadership.

- ECUSA introduced gay marriage in 2015, followed by the Canadian Episcopal Church in 2016 and the (Anglican) Church of Scotland in 2017.

- Four dioceses in the USA that were opposed to these developments withdrew from ECUSA and joined together with other dissenting congregations to form the Anglican Church of North America (ACNA), rejecting same-sex unions and the ordination of sexually active gay and lesbian people.

- Some other Anglican national churches, including Brazil, Canada, South India, and South Africa, have moved in the direction of affirming same-sex relationships. For example, in 2018, the New Zealand Synod voted in favour of allowing blessing rites for same-sex marriages and civil unions.

- In 2023, the Church of England's Synod voted to authorise a form of blessing for same-sex relationships. This move was publicly welcomed by the Archbishop of Canterbury, after which a meeting of GAFCON, reported to represent 85% of global Anglicans, resolved that the Archbishop of Canterbury's leadership in the global Anglican Communion had become "entirely indefensible".[50]

Splits have emerged in Anglican churches in every jurisdiction where national churches have moved to bless same-sex relationships. For example, the GAFCON movement consecrated the Reverend Jay Behan as a bishop to New Zealand to provide oversight for New Zealand Anglicans who no longer wish to remain with the pre-existing Anglican province. GAFCON has also consecrated a missionary bishop to Europe, the Reverend Andy Lines, after the Church of Scotland changed its church laws for marriage to include same-sex couples.

> Splits have emerged everywhere national Anglican churches have blessed same-sex relationships.

The details of the global splits are complex, and have only revealed themselves gradually through a series of incremental actions and inactions. The relative proportions of the split have also varied from country to country, reflecting the varying strengths of conservative and progressive theological positions. In some jurisdictions, there have also been painful and costly legal disputes over who gets to keep the property of congregations that choose to leave a diocese in pursuit of alternative episcopal oversight.

50 gafcon.org/news/gafcon-iv-the-kigali-commitment

Some further points need to be made about the global Anglican realignment before we consider the Australian situation. As Anglican polity is episcopal, establishing an alternative bishop for a defined region is the way splits develop, as dissenting congregations and believers seek compatible episcopal oversight. This is why the Anglican global realignment division takes the form of an alternative bishop being consecrated to a region.

In a presbyterian polity, a schism would be achieved by establishing an alternative synod or General Assembly and alternative presbyteries. In a congregational polity, a schism can simply be effected by the establishment of a new congregation, or by a congregation deciding to leave their movement.

Those who have left established denominations to join new ones do not normally consider the issue of the sinfulness of same-sex relations, or the dependent matter of acceptance of same-sex marriage, to be the main presenting issue, although it has normally been the trigger for action. Rather, the key issue has been the authority and interpretation of the Bible. Those dioceses that have affirmed same-sex relationships have a more liberal hermeneutic, giving a greater weight to culture and human judgement than more conservative approaches accept. For example, Biblical authority is emphasised as a core point of division by the GAFCON movement.

> Those who have left established denominations see the key issue to be the authority and interpretation of the Bible.

IMPLICATIONS FOR GROWTH AND DECLINE

In North America, the breakaway conservative Anglican Church of North America (ACNA) has been growing consistently, while ECUSA and the Anglican Church of Canada (ACoC), the larger continuing liberal denominations, are ageing and in decline. In the case of ECUSA, its membership took 50 years to halve, from the 1960s to the present, but at recent annual rates of decline, attendance will drop by another half in just 20 more years.

> In North America, liberal Anglican denominations are ageing and in decline.

In 2017, in three-quarters of ECUSA congregations the majority of the congregation was over 50. In the same year, two-thirds of active Episcopalian priests were 55 or older, and enrolment in seminaries had been declining.[51] In 2021, funerals outnumbered baptisms by nearly two to one, hundreds of parishes could not recruit a priest, and one in every four priests was homosexual.[52]

In contrast, ACNA is growing.[53] In 2017, it had around 16% of the attendance of ECUSA and ACoC combined, but

---

51 These statistics are taken from a variety of ECUSA reports accessed via their website: episcopalchurch.org

52 Mary Ann Mueller, "Episcopal Church: Executive Council rearranges deck chairs." *Virtue Online*, 13 June 2023. virtueonline.org/episcopal-church-executive-council-rearranges-deck-chairs

53 ACNA attendance in 2017 was 93,489. That same year, ECUSA Sunday attendance was reported to be 561,281. See Andrew Gross and Rachel Thebeau. 2017. "Congregational Report to ACNA Provincial Council." web.archive.org/web/20201112021636/episcopalchurch.org/files/documents/updated_3._average_sunday_attendance_by_province_and_diocese_2008-2018.pdf

if current trends continue, ACNA attendances will overtake ECUSA and ACoC within a generation. Thus North American Anglicans opposed to same-sex marriage are not a small splinter, but constitute a major schism.

ANGLICAN DIVISIONS

Australian Anglican dioceses are not in agreement on the issue of same-sex relations and, as has happened in other nations, the Anglican Church of Australia is steadily, if reluctantly, moving towards division over this issue.

> The Australian Anglican Church is steadily moving towards division.

In September 2019, the Synod of the Diocese of Wangaratta passed a motion to introduce a rite for blessing of same-sex marriages. In November of the same year, Newcastle Synod also made moves in this direction, and in time, other dioceses are likely to follow suit.

In response, the then Primate, Archbishop Philip Freier, requested Wangaratta not to implement the new liturgy and referred the question of the legality of this new rite to the Anglican Appellate Tribunal. A question that Freier requested the Tribunal to rule on was whether the new liturgies being proposed by Wangaratta and Newcastle were consistent with the doctrine of the Anglican Church of Australia. In November 2020, the Appellate Tribunal issued a controversial 5–1 majority opinion that the blessing of civil marriages, including same-sex marriages, is valid.

Other dioceses opposed Wangaratta's move. For example, at its annual Synod in 2019, which took place just after the Wangaratta decision, Melbourne Diocese expressed "sorrow" at Wangaratta's decision: around two-thirds of the Synod supported this motion. A similar proportion of the Melbourne Synod also expressed support for the recent consecration of Jay Behan, the GAFCON-aligned missionary bishop for New Zealand. Australia's largest Anglican diocese, the Sydney Diocese, has expressed even stronger opposition to the recent developments.

The Australian Anglican General Synod commissioned a set of essays from the Doctrine Commission, published in June 2019, entitled *Marriage, Same-Sex Marriage and the Anglican Church of Australia*. These essays reflect a variety of mutually incompatible theological views.

In 2022, the Australian Anglican General Synod dealt with a series of motions relating to same-sex marriage. A motion supporting same-sex marriage and declaring it a moral good was defeated, yet gained the support of a substantial 40% minority. An opposing motion declaring that same-sex marriage is contrary to Jesus' teachings was passed by the laity (63–47) and the clergy (70–39) but narrowly defeated by the diocesan bishops (10–12).

More significant in the longer term than the outcome of any particular motion at a single Synod gathering is the growing strength of conservatives across Australia. This trend is ultimately driven by the comparative strength of conservative parishes around the country and the decline of progressive parishes. The Appellate Tribunal's members are appointed by General

> Australian Anglican conservatives are growing in strength.

Synod, so eventually it can be expected that the theological views of Tribunal members will become more aligned with the majority view at General Synod, and the Appellate Tribunal's endorsement of same-sex marriage can be expected to be eventually overturned.

Australia is the only Western Anglosphere country whose Anglican Church has a majority of conservatives. In other nations, the progressive camp has held the majority and the conservatives have been the ones to break ranks. In Australia, it is the other way around. While the Anglican Church of Australia will continue to debate this issue, what seems very clear is that General Synod will not be endorsing same-sex relationships any time soon. The progressive cause will not, in the foreseeable future, gain enough votes to pass in that forum, the conservatives' numbers being too strong and indeed increasing while the progressives' numbers are declining.

Breakthroughs to advance full acceptance of same-sex relationships in Anglican churches will come at a diocesan level, but only in some dioceses. It seems inevitable that at some point in the near future, an Australian Diocese will fully implement a same-sex marriage rite.

> Breakthroughs on same-sex marriage will come, but only in some dioceses.

After the 2022 General Synod, and in the aftermath of the Appellate Tribunal's ruling, GAFCON stepped in to establish the Diocese of the Southern Cross in Australia in order to provide oversight to clergy and congregations who feel unable, in good conscience, to continue to serve under theologically progressive bishops or in progressive dioceses. At the time of writing, Southern Cross congregations have been established in Brisbane, Cairns, and the greater Perth area. In each case, the pastor has felt unable, in good conscience, to continue under the oversight of their bishop, because of the bishop's stance on same-sex relationships.

In other dioceses, clergy and congregations are considering their options. This is the case, for example, in Perth Diocese after the Archbishop of Perth, Kay Goldsworthy, ordained to the priesthood a man living with another man in a civil union partnership, despite receiving many formal objections from clergy and lay members of her diocese. Objections were also made to her ordaining as a deacon a man who had only recently married his long-term de facto partner, with whom he had fathered children.

Some progressives have suggested that, just as the majority of Australian Anglicans have accepted divorce and women priests, the same will inevitably happen for same-sex marriage. However, the fact that the GAFCON-affiliated Southern Cross Diocese has welcomed women priests shows that the theological fault line over same-sex marriage is different from and more difficult to overcome than differences over the ordination of women.

Despite efforts to keep the Australian Anglican Church together, at some point there will be a parting of the ways. It will be gradual, incremental, and piecemeal. The strong desire of some bishops, with the support of their dioceses, to fully welcome same-sex couples will lead them to break ranks, even if General Synod will not endorse the change. Other bishops and dioceses will maintain opposition to embracing same-sex unions. The time will come, and is already approaching, when these two views will no longer be able to be contained in the one church.

> The Anglicans' parting of the ways will be gradual, incremental, and piecemeal.

DISCIPLINE AND COMPLIANCE

The Australian Anglican Church has developed a *Faithfulness in Service* code of conduct which is used throughout Australia. According to *Faithfulness in Service*, Anglican Church workers are required to conform to the requirement to "be chaste and not engage in sex outside marriage" (§7.4).

Although this purports to be a national standard, given Australian Anglicans' episcopal polity, it is up to individual diocesan bishops whether to apply church discipline to enforce this requirement, and bishops vary in the rigour with which they discipline clergy about sexual misconduct. There is a gap between rule and practice, and compliance is not consistent. In some dioceses, partnered gay clergy occupy licensed positions in spite of the requirements of *Faithfulness in Service*, sometimes openly and sometimes covertly, with or without the knowledge or approval of the bishop;[54] but there are other diocesan bishops who refuse to license partnered gay clergy. At the same time, not all diocesan bishops withdraw the licences of clergy who commit adultery.

In a telling departure from the national standard, Perth Diocesan Synod reworded the *Faithfulness in Service* regulations in 2019 to remove the prohibition of "sex outside marriage". Instead, the

> In Perth Diocese, adultery is no longer a code of conduct violation for clergy.

---

[54] A widely publicised example is two Anglican priests, the Reverend John Davis and the Reverend Rob Whalley, who have been living together for two decades.

Perth standard requires that ministers should be "be chaste and not engage in disgraceful conduct of a sexual nature".[55]

This is a more liberal approach to sexual ethics, which downgrades the objective concept of adultery, replacing it with the subjective concept of what a community may find "disgraceful". Perth is also one of the dioceses whose Synod and bishop have been moving in the direction of blessing same-sex relationships.

This combination of tolerance for unchastity and embracing same-sex marriage illustrates an important point: that Anglican divisions are not just about homosexual relationships, but reflect a broader impact of the sexual revolution, which has influenced churchgoers' attitudes to both heterosexual and homosexual relationships.

CONCLUDING REMARKS

As we have seen, there is not a consensus among Australian Anglicans to reject the traditional view that same-sex relationships are sinful, and the traditional Christian approach to sexual ethics has not been set aside by the denomination as a whole. Nevertheless, doctrinal resistance to same-sex marriage is greater among Australian Anglicans than in these other Western nations. The Anglican General Synod is not going to affirm same-sex relationships in the foreseeable future, because progressives simply do not have

> Anglican resistance to same-sex marriage is greater in Australia than in other Western nations.

---

55 *Faithfulness in Service*, §7.4 (as amended and adopted by the Anglican Diocese of Perth in 2019).

enough votes. This is in contrast to how things have turned out in other provinces, including Canada, the USA, and New Zealand, where conservatives have been in the minority.

The percentage of those who support or oppose same-sex marriage varies from diocese to diocese across Australia. In Melbourne, around two-thirds of the 2019 Synod supported motions that in one way or another rejected same-sex marriage. On the other hand, at Wangaratta Synod in 2019, the vote in favour of a same-sex marriage rite was 78%.[56] At the Sydney Synod, a large majority is against same-sex marriage.

Support for same-sex relations is not trending in just one direction. I attended Melbourne Anglican Synods for more than 20 years, and during that time my impression was that the proportion of conservatives was slowly growing. This reflected the gradual decline in influence of progressive theological views across the diocese. On the other hand, in dioceses that are on the cutting edge of advocating for a change in sexual ethics, such as Wangaratta and Perth, the trend of the voting at Synods seems to be in the opposite direction. This is not a matter of some dioceses taking a lead and others catching up later, but of a parting of the ways. Some dioceses are going one way; others are going another way.

There are Australian Anglicans who consider same-sex relations to be prohibited by church doctrine, and there are other Australian Anglicans who see compatibility with church doctrine. These two groups, over time, will lose the will to stay together. Because

---

56 Muriel Porter. "Same-sex marriage blessing approved by synod in country Victoria." *The Melbourne Anglican,* 2 September 2019. web.archive.org/web/20211024070057/http://tma.melbourneanglican.org.au/news/same-sex-marriage-blessing-approved-wangaratta-020919

of the Anglican Church's episcopal polity, a natural point of division will be between dioceses, with some dioceses going in one direction and some going in the other, while the newly formed Diocese of the Southern Cross will pick up conservative clergy and congregations in progressive dioceses.

7

THE UNITING CHURCH

The Uniting Church in Australia (UCA) was formed in 1977 when the Australian Methodist, Congregationalist, and Presbyterian churches joined together. Although the national Synod of the Australian Presbyterian Church voted to enter the union, provision was made for individual congregations not to join but remain in a continuing Presbyterian church.[57] At the time, it was thought that the formation of the UCA would be the beginning of a movement, which other denominations might join in the future.

The Uniting Church is sometimes described, based on Australian Census data, as the nation's third-largest denomination after the Catholics and Anglicans. But in terms of weekly

---

57 Almost two thirds of Presbyterian congregations joined the union. Congregational churches, because of their congregational polity, had to opt in to join on a congregation-by-congregation basis, with 15% opting out to form the Fellowship of Congregational Churches. Methodists were offered no alternative, so congregations or individuals who did not wish to join the union had to walk away.

attendances, by 2011 it was ranked fifth, after Catholics, Pentecostals, Anglicans, and Baptists.[58]

The Uniting Church has a presbyterian polity, and is governed by four levels of assemblies:[59]

1. Congregational
2. Presbytery
3. State Synod
4. A national Assembly, meeting every three years.

Each of the six state Synods is convened by a Moderator (in an elected position), and the national Assembly is led by an elected President who serves a three-year term. The UCA is regulated by its *Constitution* and its *Basis of Union* document, which contains doctrinal statements and sets out the purpose and nature of the church, including its sources of authority.

DOCTRINE AND POLITY

The *Basis of Union* calls the books of the Old and New Testaments "unique prophetic and apostolic testimony, in which [the church] hears the Word of God and by which her faith and obedience are nourished". This is a weak statement. The Bible is not described as the Word of God, but as "testimony" through which the

> The UCA's *Basis of Union* does not regard the Bible as an authority to be obeyed.

---

58 Ruth Powell, Miriam Petter, and Sam Sterland. 2017. *How many Australians attend church in an average week?* Sydney: NCLS Research. www.ncls.org.au/articles/australians-attending-church/

59 victas.uca.org.au/about-us/our-structure

Word is heard, and the Bible itself is not described as an authority to be obeyed; rather, the heard Word nourishes obedience. Obeying commandments and having one's obedience nourished by listening to the testimony conveyed by commandments are not the same thing at all. This formulation arguably leaves the question of Biblical authority open, and intentionally so.

How is this listening process to take place? The *Basis of Union* explains that the church receives assistance in understanding these scriptures from experts it describes as "scholarly interpreters" (Paragraph 11: Scholarly Interpreters).

References in the *Basis of Union* to "councils" emphasise the role of discernment in determining what the will of God is, assuming that God speaks to the church through the church's councils. The presumption is that whatever a council decides will be the will of Christ:

> The Uniting Church acknowledges that Christ alone is supreme in his Church, and that he may speak to her through any of her councils. It is the task of every council to wait upon God's Word, and to obey his will in the matters allocated to its oversight. (*Basis of Union*, Paragraph 15: Councils)

The *Basis of Union* also emphasises that the process of discernment of God's will has a progressive[60] character, which should include openness to advances in science and contemporary thought. Its statement of the laws of the church emphasises the role of human beings in determining these laws: "since law is received by man and framed by him, it is always subject to revision", and

---

60 By "progressive" I do not mean politically left-wing, but the sense of progress developed in Kant's famous essay "What is Enlightenment?" in which he advanced the view that the "proper destiny" of humankind lies in advancement in people's ability to progress their own understanding.

"the Uniting Church will keep her law under constant review …" (Paragraph 17: The Church's Laws).

There is no concept in the *Basis of Union* of the existence of a divinely mandated moral law for humanity to follow: no reference is made to the Ten Commandments or to any other moral commandments of Jesus or the Bible that should be obeyed by Christians.

> There is no concept in the *Basis of Union* of a divinely mandated moral law.

The *Basis of Union* does make reference to historical documents, including the *Scots Confession of Faith*, the *Heidelberg Catechism*, the *Westminster Confession of Faith* and Wesley's sermons. While these had been foundational doctrinal texts for the denominations that came together to found the UCA in 1977, in the *Basis of Union* they are relegated as texts from which the Uniting Church will "continue to learn" as a "witness" from the past, and are no longer considered binding texts for church doctrine or morals.

While the need for interpretation of any text is inescapable, in the broad spectrum of Christian positions on the Bible, the UCA is at the end that downplays Biblical authority and exalts human interpretation. The *Basis of Union*'s statements about the Bible seem comparatively weak, allowing interpreters of Scripture more flexibility, and more doctrinal leeway, than most other churches. It is a Christian outlier in these respects. The *Basis of Union* also provides less guidance for Christian ethics than the constituting documents of most other churches.

Let us now turn to the UCA's *Constitution*. According to it, the state Synods have responsibility for overseeing the denomination's activities within their regions, and exercise "executive, administrative, pastoral and disciplinary functions over the Presbyteries" in supporting the church's mission. The responsibility for determining doctrine, however, is wholly in the hands of the national Assembly. The Assembly also has a power of veto over lower councils, since it can "disallow any by-law, rule or decision of a Synod or Presbytery or any other body" that contravenes the *Basis for Union* and the *Regulations* set by the Assembly. The Assembly can also create and dissolve Synods.

> In UCA polity the national Assembly determines doctrine.

UCA polity is more centralised than the Australian Anglican system. In Anglican polity, the key powers are held by bishops-in-synod at the diocesan level, and the Anglican General Synod provides an overarching framework within which the dioceses can cooperate, but General Synod cannot override the individual dioceses. Thus, a regulation passed by Anglican General Synod only applies in all of Australia if each individual diocese endorses it. In contrast, the UCA Assembly has the option to seek the agreement of the lower councils for its decisions, but it is under no obligation to do so. The Assembly also determines regulations for local churches, including rules for membership and the selection, ordination, and regulation of clergy.

In UCA polity, since the national Assembly determines doctrine, it is ultimately the body that determines the UCA's position on same-sex relationships, and it does this for all of Australia.

The question of same-sex relationships and the ordination of sexually active same-sex attracted people has been a disputed and controversial topic for the Uniting Church Assemblies

> The question of same-sex relationships has been a disputed topic for the UCA since the 1980s.

since the 1980s. In the matter of sexual ethics, there has been a gradual evolution in the Uniting Church's position: in this, it has proved to be the most progressive of major Australian Christian denominations.[61] The 2018 Assembly authorised same-sex marriages within the UCA, but left it up to the discretion of individual clergy and congregations as to whether they wished to take up this option or refuse it.[62] At the same time, the UCA has also retained the traditional heteronormative rite and doctrine of marriage, alongside the new rite and doctrine. In this way, the UCA has recognised two mutually incompatible doctrines on human sexuality and marriage, a development which received considerable media coverage at the time. The ABC reported that the Moderator of South Australia, the Reverend Sue Ellis, stated that "people who hold a conservative or traditional view of marriage, being between a man and a woman, will continue in that belief and will continue to teach and practise that belief. And those who uphold that two people can be married of any gender, will teach and practice that belief and continue it."[63]

The 2018 decision of the UCA Assembly implied that the doctrine of the Uniting Church can embrace both sides of the

---

[61] web.archive.org/web/20201130174919/assembly.uca.org.au/resources/marriage/item/2824-history

[62] web.archive.org/web/20230312131115/https://assembly.uca.org.au/news/item/2854-freedom-to-decide-on-marriage

[63] Ben Nielsen. "Uniting Church to continue to allow same-sex marriages following deciding vote in SA." *ABC News*, 7 January 2019. abc.net.au/news/2019-01-07/uniting-church-to-allow-same-sex-marriages-after-deciding-vote/10692284

theological dispute, so that for Uniting Church members and ministers, it is doctrinally equally acceptable to accept or reject same-sex relations. Although this solution is in tension with the *Basis of Union*'s contention that Synod's role is to discern the will of God about matters (Paragraph 15: Councils), it aligns with its statement that the laws of the church are subject to change and fashioned by humans for humans.

This decision implies either that there is no such thing as God's truth on this issue—only different human interpretations, which must be treated as equally valid—or that the Christian understanding of marriage is a lower-order issue which is of insufficient weight to justify division.

Of course, in any denomination there will be doctrinal matters on which people disagree. As someone once said to me about the Anglican Church: "It is wonderful belonging to a church in which you can believe one thing one day and something else the next." The point of this seemingly flippant remark was not that all beliefs are equal, but that there are matters of belief on which people can legitimately disagree, and even change their minds, without changing their church.

> In any denomination there will be doctrines people disagree on.

In the half-century since the union, theologically conservative[64] congregations have been leaving the UCA, and even today, not all UCA congregations support its theologically progressive trend. In particular, the many ethnic congregations established by immigrants from the Global South are more theologically

---

64   Within the UCA context, theological conservatives typically identify as evangelicals.

conservative and younger than the ageing, progressive Anglo UCA congregations.

In 2006, the Assembly of Confessing Congregations was formed within the Uniting Church[65] to resist and oppose the progressive trend within the UCA. In 2021, the Tongan–Australian chair of the Assembly of Confessing Congregations, Hedley Fihaki,[66] had his recognition as a minister withdrawn by the UCA for communications that did not show respect for the UCA's leaders and decisions. In March 2023, his former congregation, Mooloolaba Christian Church, was also dissolved by the local UCA Presbytery.

The Assembly of Confessing Congregations voted to cease its operations in 2023, and the breakaway Anglican Diocese of the Southern Cross has now recognised eight former UCA ministers as ordained Anglican clergy. The former members of Mooloolaba Christian Church, now rebranded as Faith Church, have joined Southern Cross Diocese under the leadership of the Reverend Fihaki, who is now licensed as an Anglican priest.

Not all theological conservatives in the Uniting Church are ready to leave. A way forward for some has been to stay in the denomination while establishing networks and assemblies of like-minded people. The discontinued Assembly of

> Not all UCA theological conservatives are ready to leave.

---

65 https://web.archive.org/web/20220309104311/https://confessingcongregations.org.au/

66 See these two reports for a list of charges against the Reverend Fihaki and a UCA statement: theothercheek.com.au/uniting-church-why-we-removed-hedley-fihaki-as-a-minister
theothercheek.com.au/evangelical-minister-hedley-fihaki-reveals-the-uniting-church-charges-that-led-to-his-removal

Confessing Congregations was one such attempt, but others continue, such as the evangelical Propel Network,[67] and in South Australia, the non-geographical evangelical Generate Presbytery[68] supports 115 UCA congregations and ministries.

DISCIPLINE AND COMPLIANCE

The Uniting Church *Regulations*, as determined by the national Assembly, provide detailed guidelines for responding to and handling allegations of sexual misconduct against church members. However, neither the *Regulations* nor the UCA's *Code of Ethics and Ministry Practice* make any reference to chastity, extramarital sex, or homosexuality. In the UCA's *Regulations*, the definition of "sexual misconduct" addresses principles of professional sexual ethics only: there is no prohibition of sex outside marriage, whether homosexual or heterosexual.[69]

It appears that the Ten Commandments' prohibition of adultery does not apply to Uniting Church members, for the UCA's *Regulations* offer no capacity to discipline clergy who break their marriage vows. If a pastor had an adulterous relationship, this would not be considered a breach of the church's codes, so long as the relationship was lawful and not unprofessional.

> The UCA is not bound by the Ten Commandments' prohibition of adultery.

---

67 propelnetwork.org.au

68 generate.ucasa.org.au

69 This is not to imply that adultery is approved of by UCA members or presbyteries.

To be consistent and treat people fairly, a denomination should have just one code of conduct, not multiple, competing, and conflicting codes. One of the problems with the UCA's "dual doctrines" approach is that the denomination could not conceivably provide dual patterns of church discipline to match their dual doctrines. Yet, to hold to a doctrine means there needs to be a potential to apply discipline accordingly. It is to be expected that a denomination that embraces same-sex marriage would discipline a pastor who preaches against it, while a denomination that accepts only heterosexual marriage would discipline a pastor who preaches in favour of same-sex marriage.[70] It will simply not be feasible to apply conflicting "dual disciplines" in the one denomination to accommodate these two opposing positions.

In reality, the UCA's *Regulations* favour progressive sexual ethics, since there is no prohibition of unchastity or adultery, to there are no "dual ethics" to match the "dual doctrines" marriage policy.

---

[70] An example of the former from the UK was the sacking in 2019 of the Reverend Bernard Randle from his position as a chaplain at Trent College, a Church of England school, after he gave a sermon in which he said that it was acceptable for students to hold traditional views on marriage, sex and gender identity. He was declared to be a "moderate risk to children". See Sophie Drew. "Christian chaplain sacked for marriage comments claims he was 'blacklisted' by Church of England safeguarding." *Premier Christian News*, 6 September 2022. premierchristian.news/us/news/article/christian-chaplain-sacked-for-marriage-comments-claims-he-was-blacklisted-by-church-of-england-safeguarding

8

TWO PENTECOSTAL MOVEMENTS

The global phenomenon of Pentecostalism arose from revival movements at the end of the 19th century and the beginning of the 20th century, including the 1904–1905 Welsh Revival and the Azusa Street Revival of 1905–1916 in Los Angeles. The founder of the first Pentecostal church in Australia was a woman, Sarah Jane Lancaster, who opened the Good News Hall in North Melbourne in 1909.

Multiple Pentecostal movements have been active in Australia, of which the largest is Australian Christian Churches (formerly known as the Assemblies of God). Others include the International Network of Churches (formerly the Christian Outreach Centre), CRC Churches International (formerly the Christian Revival Crusade), and Global Acts Churches (formerly the Apostolic Church Australia), and C3 Church Global (formerly known as Christian City Church International).[71] All these movements have

---

71 Rebranding is common among Pentecostal churches.

experienced significant growth during the 20th century and into this century, bucking the trend of Western Christian decline.

As I have noted, Australian Census data are not a reliable indication of the strength of the Pentecostal movement. Despite Pentecostals being the second-largest Christian grouping after the Catholics in terms of active membership, there is no "Pentecostal" box in the Census for people to tick. Some Pentecostals will tick "Other" under the Christian category and not necessarily write "Pentecostal". Some who attend Pentecostal churches may tick a denomination such as "Baptist" or "Lutheran", matching their earlier pattern of worship or the denomination into which they were baptised or the faith of their family of origin. Or they might just write "Christian", as that would in any case be a more accurate description of their religious identity than "Pentecostal".

By and large, both secular Australian society and the traditional denominations have been slow to grasp the transformative significance of the growth of Pentecostal movements for Australian Christianity.

> Some have been slow to grasp the significance of the growth of Pentecostal movements in Australia.

Running parallel to the Pentecostal movement has been the Charismatic movement, a multi-streamed spiritual renewal movement within traditional denominations which shares many Pentecostal emphases. The Charismatic movement began in the late 1950s and became a significant influence upon mainstream churches during the 1970s. It has been estimated that around one-quarter of Christians in the world are Pentecostals or Charismatics.

Often meeting in school halls or converted factories, Pentecostals do not rely on a history of social privilege or imposing architecture. They do not rely on the cultural trappings of Christianity. Instead, Pentecostal churches tend to be highly culturally adaptive, although conservative in doctrine and ethics. An example of their cultural adaptivity—in addition to all the rebranding—is the shift in church worship music away from hymns and choruses towards rock-style bands, which has also influenced many non-Pentecostal congregations.

> Pentecostals tend to be highly culturally adaptive, but conservative in doctrine and ethics.

While traditional denominations have been declining, Pentecostals have been busy planting churches. Pentecostals have a younger demographic than the more established denominations. A common pattern in suburbs and country towns across Australia is that there will be a handful of declining, elderly mainstream Protestant churches in the town, and one or more dynamic, growing, and youthful Pentecostal churches.

In the following sections, we will consider two Australian Pentecostal denominations, one large and one small.

AUSTRALIAN CHRISTIAN CHURCHES

Australian Christian Churches (ACC) is Australia's largest Pentecostal movement, with over 1,000 churches and more than 3,000 pastors. There are more ACC members than Anglicans attending church each week, which makes ACC the second-largest Christian movement in Australia after the Catholic Church.

Most Pentecostal movements have congregational governance, and this is the approach of ACC. Each individual ACC congregation is self-governing, but constituent congregations must endorse the movement's vision and policies and be committed to work in missional partnership with other ACC movement churches.

ACC's doctrinal statement, contained within its *United Constitution*, is brief at around 750 words, in contrast to the Catholic *Catechism*'s 848 pages and the Anglican Church of North America's 160-page catechism. The first point in the doctrinal statement is that "The Holy Scriptures, known as the Bible, is the inspired Word of God and our all sufficient rule for faith and practice", and all the other points are "grounded in these scriptures". Apart from this point, the doctrinal statement has next to nothing to say about ethics: the statement does not refer to God's laws, the Ten Commandments, or loving others. Nevertheless, one can rightly conclude from the phrase "and practice" that the ACC considers the Bible to be the foundational guide for Christian ethics. However, the way that is construed is left up to individual congregations to interpret, except that the ACC's *Ministerial Code of Conduct* goes into some detail about the behaviour expected of ACC ministers.

> The ACC takes the Bible to be the foundational guide for Christian ethics.

ACC credentials ministers who have been ordained by their congregations. To be credentialed, someone must accept ACC's *United Constitution*, including the doctrinal statement; comply with the policies of the movement; and, for ministers, live consistently with the movement's *Ministerial Code of Conduct*. This code declares that "homosexual behaviour is forbidden by

Scripture (Romans 1:24–25)". It further upholds "chastity in singleness and faithfulness in marriage".

The ACC's *United Constitution* and *Ministerial Code of Conduct* can only be changed by the National Conference, which is the "supreme governing body" of the movement.[72] The National Conference consists of representatives of the churches in the movement, together with credentialed ordained ministers. Each congregation has one voting delegate for every 250 adults who regularly attend, and each ordained minister is entitled to one vote. In April 2021, the ACC National Conference was attended by 1800 delegates.[73]

Amendments to the *United Constitution* must receive a majority vote of 75% of delegates, while amendments to policies, including the *Ministerial Code of Conduct*, require a 65% majority vote.

ACC has a hybrid governance system. The fundamental organisation is congregational: each congregation chooses voluntarily to affiliate with ACC. If an individual church desired, for example, to celebrate same-sex marriages, it could easily leave the movement, freeing itself from all ACC requirements. Property is owned at the congregational level, not by the denomination, and pastors are employed locally, not centrally. However, as far as ACC's doctrine and ethics are concerned, a Presbyterian-like system of authority applies, with parameters being set by the National Conference, and the majority required to bring about change at that level is high.

There is no evidence that any changes to the ACC *Ministerial Code of Conduct*'s definitions of marriage and chastity are presently

---

72 *United Constitution*, §51.
73 Australian Christian Churches. "Prime Minister Addresses Delegates." April 2021. acc.org.au/news-media/acc-national-conference-2021

being considered. Unlike the UCA, the ACC has no history of considering proposals to embrace same-sex relationships. This is consistent with the conservative views of most Pentecostal believers.

> The ACC has no history of proposals to embrace same-sex relationships.

Although ACC holds to a conservative Christian position about same-sex relationships, and National Church Life Survey data show that Australian Pentecostals have the most conservative views about sexuality, most ACC churches have preferred to keep a low public profile on this issue. This was apparent during the public debates about introducing same-sex marriage, and it aligns with a tendency for Pentecostals to avoid partisan political activism, which American missiologist Peter Wagner has called a "social strike".[74]

DISCIPLINE AND COMPLIANCE

ACC has the capacity, through its *Ministerial Code of Conduct*, to discipline pastors for breaches of sexual ethics such as adultery or homosexual activity. When such matters arise, the State Executive becomes involved and a decredentialing process can be initiated. Ultimately, the decision to decredential would be made at the level of the National Executive.

ACC has a track record of disciplining pastors for breaches of the *Code*. Normally, the movement initiates not only a decredentialing process but also a rehabilitation process, if the person who is in breach of the *Code* wishes to repent.

---

74 C. Peter Wagner. 1973. *Look out! The Pentecostals Are Coming*. Carol Stream, IL: Creation House.

ACTS GLOBAL CHURCHES

Acts Global Churches is a smaller Australian Pentecostal movement which traces its roots back to the Welsh Revival. Globally, the movement is known as the Apostolic Church, a label shared by a number of diverse and unrelated denominations around the world. Today the largest national Apostolic Church is in Nigeria. In Australia, there are around 100 congregations in the Acts Global movement, around a tenth the number of ACC congregations.

The Welsh antecedent to the Australian Apostolic movement adopted a Presbyterian governance. However, today Acts Global Churches has what is in effect an episcopal polity, but without a "bishop".

The Apostolic Church movement emphasises the gifting of the Holy Spirit for apostolic leadership. In this sense, leaders are chosen by God and discerned by the church. In Acts Global Churches, authority comes from the top down as in an episcopal system. Authority rests with the National Leader and their Leadership Team. It is the National Leader, together with the National Leadership Team of eight men and women, who appoints pastors of local churches.

> In Acts Global Churches, authority rests with the National Leader and their Leadership Team.

In contrast to ACC, all Acts Global Churches property is owned centrally by a national property trust. Financial accounts are also owned by the movement, not by local churches, and payroll is run centrally. The legal entity that manages property, finances, and employment for the movement is a company limited by guarantee, "Acts Global Churches Limited".

Alongside the National Leadership Team, a group of senior ministers, known as the National Eldership, has the sole function of appointing both the National Leader, who serves for a two-year term, and the members of the National Leadership Team.

The National Leadership Team is assisted by Network Leaders, who support local churches and their pastors.

The Acts Global Churches *Statement of Belief* is relatively short at 246 words, a third the length of the ACC statement. There is nothing in this statement about ethics.

The statement can be updated when required by the National Leadership Team, but this has rarely been needed. However, in recent years, the *Statement of Belief* was altered to add an additional clause: "We believe that the covenant of marriage is the union of a man and a woman who have voluntarily entered into a loving, committed and exclusive relationship for as long as both live." No doubt this was added as a protective measure in case a court or tribunal wishes to determine what the movement's doctrine is on marriage for the purposes of anti-discrimination law.

> There are no moves within Acts Global to endorse same-sex relationships.

The Acts Global movement's Leadership Team has adopted *Conditions of Service and Certification*, which is a code of conduct for pastors. These conditions describe as misconduct "intimate sexual relationship with any person other than spouse".

Like ACC, Acts Global's theological statement emphasises "the Divine inspiration and authority of the Holy Scripture", and there are no moves within Acts Global Churches to endorse same-sex relationships. In their sexual conservatism, ACC and Acts Global Churches are very similar, despite their very different polities.

DISCIPLINE AND COMPLIANCE

Acts Global Churches have the capacity and willingness to decredential pastors who are in breach of the movement's code of conduct. One of the *Conditions of Service and Certification* is that "the minister agrees that the Church may change the nature of, or terminate a ministry certificate and/or employment in the event of misconduct".

The National Leader would make the decision to decredential, in consultation with the National Leadership Team. As with ACC, steps would normally also be taken to attempt the rehabilitation of a pastor who has been decredentialed.

9

TWO REFORMED DENOMINATIONS

Churches in the Reformed tradition identify with the teachings and theology of John Calvin. Although Reformed churches can have episcopal, presbyterian, or congregational polity, the two denominations we shall consider here have presbyterian polity. These are the larger Presbyterian Church, which derives from the Scottish Reformed tradition, and the small Free Reformed Church of Australia, which derives from the Dutch Reformed tradition.

THE PRESBYTERIAN CHURCH OF AUSTRALIA

The Presbyterian Church of Australia (PCA) is the largest Reformed church in Australia. It derives from Scottish roots and has over 50,000 enrolled members.

The PCA was formed in 1901 when the Presbyterian state churches came together. In 1977, around two-thirds of Presbyterian congregations joined the Uniting Church. Those who did not join continued in the PCA, not wishing to join the

UCA because of its liberal theological views. Unsurprisingly, the remnant PCA became more theologically conservative, as shown by its repeal of approval for the ordination of women in 1991.

> After the UCA was formed, the PCA became more theologically conservative.

The PCA has retained its adherence to the *Westminster Confession of Faith*, a detailed statement of around 12,000 words, as an "subordinate standard" with the Bible as the "supreme standard". All PCA ministers are required to assent to the precepts of the *Westminster Confession*.

The PCA has a presbyterian polity. Each congregation elects elders to govern it. Among these, the minister of a church is known as a *teaching elder*. The collective of congregational elders is known as the *session*. The session oversees all ministry in the church, including services and Sunday School, and approves leaders of church activities, including the minister.

In addition to the session, congregations have a committee of management which oversees church property and finances.

Above the congregation there is a body known as a Presbytery, to which each congregation contributes their minister and one other elder. The Presbytery oversees doctrinal and disciplinary issues that arise in congregations. It acts as a court for matters within its jurisdiction. It also supervises appointments and receives the resignations of ministers. Some key responsibilities of a bishop in an episcopal system are exercised by the Presbytery.

Above the Presbytery, the PCA has State Assemblies, each chaired by a Moderator. The Assembly is the highest court in each state.

At the national level, the General Assembly consists of representatives from every Presbytery and from the State Assemblies. It is the highest court of appeal in Australia for disputes that have not been able to be resolved at the Presbytery and State levels.

The State and National Assemblies have *Code Books* which function as the constitution for the denomination in the state or nation. The Code Book of the General Assembly of Australia declares that "all sexual activity outside of marriage is prohibited", and that "marriage is to be between one man and one woman". This Code Book cites the Bible and the *Westminster Confession* as its authorities for these statements: the *Westminster Confession* states that "marriage is to be between one man and one woman".

> The PCA General Assembly *Code Book* prohibits sex outside marriage.

It is striking that the PCA has maintained a conservative theological stance on Biblical authority and human sexuality while the (Presbyterian) Church of Scotland and the Presbyterian Church (USA) have embraced more liberal views, including allowing same-sex marriages to be performed in their churches. Like Anglicans, Presbyterians in Australia are more conservative than their counterparts elsewhere in the Anglosphere.

> Presbyterians in Australia are more conservative than their counterparts elsewhere.

DISCIPLINE AND COMPLIANCE

The PCA takes church discipline seriously. Indeed, it emphasises it. The booklet *An Introduction to the Presbyterian*

Church of Australia includes a section on "Discipline", which states that:

> From time to time it might be necessary for courts of the Church to act in a disciplinary way. Procedures for Discipline are set out clearly in a separate document called The Code of Discipline. Anyone wishing to study that document should ask a minister or the clerk of the local Session or Presbytery for a copy. The Code of Discipline sets out its approach to discipline in the following way:
>
> "Discipline is exercised by those appointed to rule in the Church for the glory of God, the purity of the Church and the spiritual good of the offender. Discipline is to be administered in a spirit of faithfulness, love and tenderness." (Code of Discipline 1.02)

In 1993, the Reverend Peter Cameron, a PCA minister, was found guilty of heresy for a sermon in which he supported the ordination of women, criticised the PCA's teachings on homosexuality, and declared, referring to 1 Timothy 2:11–15, that St Paul "got it wrong". After being convicted of heresy, Cameron resigned his ministry in Australia and returned to Scotland.

> In 1993 the PCA found the Revd Peter Cameron guilty of heresy.

THE FREE REFORMED CHURCH OF AUSTRALIA

In the 2016 Australian Census, 2,355 people wrote down "Free Reformed" as their religion. The website of the Free Reformed Church of Australia (FRCA) reports 17 congregations spread around Australia, of which 14 are in Western Australia.

This denomination is a Protestant church in the Dutch Reformed tradition. It has a presbyterian polity. Its General Assembly, termed a Synod, meets every three years and is attended by delegates who include an equal number of ordained ministers and lay elders, all male. The FRCA has three presbyteries, which it calls *classis*: Classis North, Classic Central, and Classis South West. The congregational-level assembly is called a *consistory*. The Synod has jurisdiction over the classis, and the classis has jurisdiction over the consistory.[75]

The FRCA is on the conservative end of Reformed churches. It does not admit women to the leadership roles of deacon, elder, or minister, and all hymns sung in churches have to be approved by the national Synod.

As its doctrinal base, the FRCA adheres to the Apostle's Creed, the Nicene Creed, and the Athanasian Creed, as well as the Three Forms of Unity, a collective term for three historical doctrinal statements: the *Canons of Dort*, the *Belgic Confessions*, and the *Heidelberg Catechism*, which are foundational for the Dutch Reformed tradition.

The *Heidelberg Catechism* defines faith as "a sure knowledge whereby I accept as true all that God has revealed to us in His Word" (i.e. in the Bible). The *Belgic Confession* contains the following statement on the authority and sufficiency of the Bible:

> Article 7—The Sufficiency of Scripture
>
> We believe that this Holy Scripture contains the will of God completely and that everything one must believe to be saved is sufficiently taught in it.
>
> …

---

75 *Church Order of the Free Reformed Churches of Australia*, Article 35.

Therefore we must not consider human writings—no matter how holy their authors may have been—equal to the divine writings; nor may we put custom, nor the majority, nor age, nor the passage of times or persons, nor councils, decrees, or official decisions above the truth of God, for truth is above everything else.

Concerning human sexuality, the *Heidelberg Catechism* includes the following statements, including an interpretation of the commandment "Do not commit adultery":

87 Q. Can those be saved who do not turn to God from their ungrateful and impenitent ways?

> A. By no means. Scripture tells us that no unchaste person, no idolater, adulterer, thief, no covetous person, no drunkard, slanderer, robber, or the like is going to inherit the kingdom of God.[1]
>
> 1. 1 Corinthians 6:9–10; Galatians 5:19–21; Ephesians 5:1–20; 1 John 3:14

108 Q. What is God's will for us in the seventh[76] commandment?

> A. God condemns all unchastity.[1] We should therefore thoroughly detest it[2] and, married or single, live decent and chaste lives.[3]
>
> 1. Leviticus 18:30; Ephesians 5:3–5
> 2. Jude 22–23
> 3. 1 Corinthians 7:1–9; 1 Thessalonians 4:3–8; Hebrews 13:4

---

76 "Do not commit adultery." I have earlier referred to this as the sixth commandment. The numbering of the commandments varies between denominations.

109 Q. Does God, in this commandment, forbid only such scandalous sins as adultery?

> A. We are temples of the Holy Spirit, body and soul, and God wants both to be kept clean and holy. That is why He forbids everything which incites unchastity,[1] whether it be actions, looks, talk, thoughts, or desires.[2]
>
> 1. 1 Corinthians 15:33; Ephesians 5:18
> 2. Matthew 5:27–29; 1 Corinthians 6:18–20; Ephesians 5:3–4

These statements forbid sexual relationships outside (heterosexual) marriage, including "actions, looks, talk, thoughts, or desires"—in other words, not only adulterous acts, but also the toleration of any sexual desire which extends beyond the boundaries of marriage. Furthermore, Article 87 states that an unrepentant adulterer cannot be saved.

> "He (God) forbids everything which incites unchastity".
> – *Heidelberg Catechism*

The cited Biblical references are key to the interpretation of these articles. For Article 109, which extends the seventh commandment beyond the actual commission of adultery, Matthew 5:27–29 is cited:

> "You have heard that it was said, 'You shall not commit adultery.' But I tell you that anyone who looks at a woman lustfully has already committed adultery with her in his heart. If your right eye causes you to stumble, gouge it out and throw it away. It is better for you to lose one part of your body than for your whole body to be thrown into hell." (New International Version)

The Greek phrase *emoicheusen autēn*, normally translated as 'committed adultery with her', is more accurately rendered as 'debauched her' or 'adulterated her marriage'. This escalation of ethics by Jesus, extending the commandment to encompass a prohibition even on entertaining lustful thoughts, is characteristic both of Jesus' teachings in the Sermon on the Mount (Matthew 5–7) and of the Reformed tradition of ethics. For example, the *Heidelberg Catechism* states, concerning the ninth commandment ("Do not bear false witness"), that it is not enough to avoid telling lies; one must also avoid any conduct which could be deceptive, and love the truth, openly confessing it:

> [The aim of the ninth commandment is] That I never give false testimony against anyone, twist no one's words, not gossip or slander, nor join in condemning anyone rashly or without a hearing. Rather, in court and everywhere else, I should avoid lying and deceit of every kind; these are the very devices the devil uses, and they would call down on me God's intense wrath. I should love the truth, speak it candidly, and openly acknowledge it. And I should do what I can to guard and advance my neighbour's good name.

This point is made to emphasise that the *Heidelberg Catechism*'s treatment of adultery is not just concerned with sexual acts, but includes a prohibition of all sexual impurity, including entertaining lustful thoughts and desires which do not conform to a Biblical standard of chastity. This is also the approach taken by the Catholic *Catechism*.

> Both the *Heidelberg Catechism* and the Catholic *Catechism* interpret the seventh commandment, "do not commit adultery", very broadly.

Article 28 of the *Belgic Confession* is also relevant. It obligates Christians to "join and unite with" the church of Christ, "keeping the unity of the church by submitting to its instruction and discipline, by bending their necks under the yoke of Jesus Christ ... even if civil authorities and royal decrees forbid and death and physical punishment result."

This means that members of the FRCA, as a body that considers the *Belgic Confession* as foundational, are obligated to submit to the teaching and discipline of the denomination, even if the law of the land prohibits it.

DISCIPLINE AND COMPLIANCE

The FRCA *Church Order* policy, Article 77, includes fornication and adultery as "serious and gross sins" which are grounds for excommunication of office-bearers. This would apply to both heterosexual and homosexual fornication or adultery, and to lay people as well as pastors. It is also clear from their Synod reports that the denomination is willing and ready to impose church discipline for sexual misdemeanours.

This concludes my discussion of a variety of church denominations and movements. In the next chapter, we will consider the results of surveys of congregants' views on sexuality.

10

THE STATE OF THE CHURCHES

In this chapter we will consider the results of surveys of Australian churchgoers concerning their attitudes to different aspects of human sexuality. Most of the data we will examine here are a decade or so old, but it is suggested that the patterns they reveal will be enduring ones.

NCLS Research is a charity that conducts research into the state and health of Australian churches. One of the ways it does this is through a survey of churchgoers conducted every five years, known as the *National Church Life Survey*. Individual churches can choose to contract with NCLS Research to provide a survey of their members who happen to be attending church during a particular week of the year. After the survey, churches receive a profile report, the Church Life Profile, containing information that can be used to assist in pursuing the church's mission.

> NCLS Research conducts research into the state and health of Australian churches.

In 2014, NCLS Research investigated what Australian churchgoers think about human sexuality, using data from their 2011 congregational survey. This chapter presents an overview of their findings.

It must be emphasised that these figures reflect the views of people attending church—that is, of more committed members—not nominal Christians who might tick a denominational Census box. There would have been some individuals who just happened to be visitors on the day when the NCLS survey was conducted, for whatever reason, and were not Christians, let alone members; however, the large majority of those polled would have been committed, regular Christian worshippers.

ADULTERY

The NCLS found that in 2011, 96.8% of people attending church believed that adultery (extramarital sex involving a married person) is always or almost always wrong. Only 0.5% believed it is not wrong.[77]

It is striking that young adults (20–30 years old at the time) had the highest proportion of those who believed extramarital sex is always wrong (97%). Baby Boomers (then 60–69 years old) had the lowest percentage who believed

> Young adults had the highest proportion who believed extramarital sex is always wrong.

---

77 Nicole Hancock, Miriam Pepper, and Ruth Powell. 2014. *Attitudes to Extra-Marital Sex*. NCLS Research Fact Sheet 14014. Sydney: NCLS Research.

extramarital sex is always wrong (84%). This is a significant finding, for it might be assumed that attitudes towards sex are becoming more liberal over time so younger people would have more liberal sexual ethics than older people. Not so—at least, not for churchgoers. The Baby Boomer Christians, who went through the sexual revolution of the 1960s and 1970s, have attitudes to sex that are more liberal than the generations that precede and follow them.

> Boomer Christians had more liberal views on sex than the generations which preceded and followed them.

We will see this trend for younger people to have more conservative attitudes on sex replicated across the other survey data discussed below. One possible explanation is that theologically conservative churches, such as the Pentecostals, attract more young people. As a rule of thumb, declining and dying churches with ageing demographics are more liberal in their ethics and theology, while growing, younger churches are more conservative in ethics and theology (but not necessarily in cultural expression).

Another finding reported by NCLS Research is that people who attended church less frequently or who practised private devotions, such as prayer and Bible study, less frequently were also less likely to believe that extramarital sex is always wrong. The more you practise your Christianity, the more likely you are to object to adultery.

> The more you practice Christianity, the more likely you are to believe extramarital sex is wrong.

The survey also found that views of church attenders on extramarital sex have "remained remarkably stable over time", there being almost no difference between the 2001 and 2011 results.

Uniting Church attenders were found to be the most permissive and Pentecostal attenders the most conservative. The ranking of the "always wrong" responses by denomination was Pentecostal (98%) > Baptist/Church of Christ (97%) > Other Protestant (95%) > Lutheran (91%) > Anglican (90%) > Catholic (84%) > Uniting (80%).

By and large, the attitudes of churchgoers match the teaching and conduct of the denominations. For example, Pentecostals' strict approach to adultery as a code of conduct breach matches their attenders' attitudes, and the Uniting Church's tolerant approach to sexual ethics in their code of conduct is matched by greater acceptance of adultery among the membership. However, there is a mismatch between the strictness of the Catholic *Catechism* on sexual ethics and the permissive attitude of many Catholics in the pews. We will see these patterns repeated for other attitudes of attenders.

> Attitudes of churchgoers tend to match the teaching and conduct of their denomination.

It should not be assumed that all Catholics hold more liberal views. There is a substantial proportion of Catholics who hold conservative views on sexual ethics, including many young Catholics, but they are a minority.

SEX BEFORE MARRIAGE

Views on sex before marriage were more permissive than for adultery. 48.6% said it was "always wrong". However, 27.4% said it was not wrong if long-term: cohabiting is more acceptable than casual sex.[78]

The age correlations for this were more complex than for adultery. As for adultery, 20–29-year-olds had the highest "always wrong" response (58%). In general, the younger the cohort, the more likely they were to consider sex before marriage as "always wrong". However, the 80+ (Builder) generation (at 57% "always wrong") were more conservative than 60–79-year-olds (40–43% "always wrong") and teenagers were not as conservative as the younger adults above them.

As for adultery, more infrequent attendance or devotional practice was associated with more liberal views.

Also as for adultery, the Pentecostals were the most conservative and the Uniting Church the most permissive. In order, the ranking of "always wrong" responses from highest to lowest was: Pentecostal (85%) > Other Protestant (70%) > Baptist/Church of Christ (69%) > Anglican (45%) > Lutheran (39%) > Catholic (34%) > Uniting (32%).

> Pentecostals were the most conservative and Uniting Church attenders the most permissive.

---

78 Nicole Hancock, Miriam Pepper, and Ruth Powell. 2014. *Attitudes to Sex Before Marriage*. NCLS Research Fact Sheet 14013. Sydney: NCLS Research.

It is striking that the ranking of the denominations is almost the same for views about adultery and sex outside marriage. The only variation was that, in relation to adultery, Lutherans are slightly more conservative than Anglicans, but on the question of sex before marriage, Anglicans are more conservative than Lutherans.

SAME-SEX MARRIAGE

In 2011, a majority (73%) of churchgoers disagreed with same-sex marriage. Most of these (56%) "strongly disagreed". In every age group, a majority disagreed with same-sex marriage, with the lowest level of disagreement being among those aged 15–19 (56% disagreement).[79]

The less often people attended church, the more likely they were to agree with same-sex marriage. This parallels the earlier observation that the more someone practises their Christianity, the more conservative their sexual ethics will be.

> The less often people attended church, the more likely they were to agree with same-sex marriage.

By denomination, the percentages who "disagreed" or "strongly disagreed" with same-sex marriage were: Other Protestant (91%), Pentecostal (88%) > Baptist/Church of Christ (85%) > Anglicans (76%) > Lutheran (75%) > Catholic (64%) > Uniting (56%).

The percentages of those who "agreed" or "strongly agreed" were: Other Protestant (3%) < Pentecostal (5%) < Baptist/Church

---

79 Nicole Hancock, Miriam Pepper, and Ruth Powell. 2014. *Attitudes to Same-Sex Marriage and Civil Unions*. NCLS Research Fact Sheet 14015. Sydney: NCLS Research.

of Christ (9%) < Anglican and Lutheran (13%) < Catholic (16%) < Uniting (26%).

SAME-SEX ADOPTION

In 2011, the NCLS also surveyed attitudes of churchgoers to same-sex adoption. People who practised their faith more frequently were less likely to approve of same-sex adoption and more likely to disapprove, and a similar pattern of acceptance across the denominations was observed to the questions on sexual ethics. Percentages of churchgoers who disapproved of same-sex adoption were: Other Protestant (85%) > Pentecostal (84%) > Baptist/Church of Christ (82%) > Lutheran (76%) > Anglican (72%) > Catholic (64%) > Uniting (62%).[80]

SUMMARY OF SURVEYS

In summary, although Australian churchgoers differed on sexual ethics, in 2011 a majority held conservative views consistent with traditional church teachings. For all issues considered, the more churchgoers practise their faith, the more conservative their views on sexuality are. It is also striking that the ranking of denominations was consistent across the different issues:

> The ranking of denominations on a conservative-progressive spectrum was consistent across the different issues.

---

[80] Nicole Hancock, Miriam Pepper, and Ruth Powell. 2014. *Attitudes to Same-Sex Adoption*. NCLS Research Fact Sheet 14012. Sydney: NCLS Research.

- The most liberal views are found among Uniting Church attenders.
- Churchgoing Catholics are liberal, but not so liberal as the Uniting Church worshippers.
- Anglican and Lutheran views are in the middle: not as liberal as Catholics, but not as conservative as other Protestants.
- Baptists, Church of Christ, Other Protestants, and Pentecostals are the most conservative. The precise ranking at the conservative end of the spectrum varies slightly depending on the issue, but overall the Pentecostals hold the most conservative views.

There is a correlation between declining attendance and progressivism. Attenders at growing churches (e.g. Pentecostals and Other Protestants) hold more conservative views on sexuality, while attenders at declining churches (e.g. the Uniting Church and the Catholic Church) hold more liberal views. The correlation between theological progressivism and church decline is a worldwide phenomenon. As Ross Douthat, writing for the *New York Times*, put it:

> It's not that conservative churches inevitably grow while liberal ones shrink; plenty of doctrinally conservative forms of Christianity have suffered buffets or declines, and there is certainly no simple "conservative" solution for secularization. But the decline of belief and practice, rather than resilience or revival, in the Christian churches that have gone farthest with the liberal program is one of the most salient facts of contemporary religious history in both America and Europe.[81]

81 Ross Douthat, "Why I'm not a liberal Catholic." *The New York Times*, 23 June 2023. nytimes.com/2023/06/23/opinion/liberal-catholic.html

There is also an approximate correlation between higher rates of nominalism—reflected in the Census box tickers who do not attend church— and more progressive sexual ethics. This same correlation can be observed within individual denominations. For example, in 2011, a "Census Anglican" was five times as likely to be in church on a Sunday morning in the conservative Sydney Diocese than in the progressive Brisbane Diocese.[82]

> Higher rates of nominalism correlate with more progressive sexual ethics.

The NCLS results for the Uniting Church are consistent with the lack of references to specific moral commandments in its *Basis of Union*—for example, there is no mention of the Ten Commandments—as well as the lack of inclusion of adultery as a form of sexual misconduct in the Uniting Church's *Regulations*. Nonetheless, in the 2011 NCLS, there was still a significant proportion of Uniting Church attenders who held more conservative views on sexuality.

The Catholic Church manifests the greatest gap between official church doctrine, which remains conservative, and the opinions of people in the pews, which include many who are towards the more liberal end of the spectrum of Australian churches. The Australian Catholic Church is officially conservative but has a significant number of progressively minded members.

The position of the Anglicans in the middle on a range of views reflects a divided rather than a homogeneous church. In recent

---

82 See the report to General Synod of the Viability and Structures Task Force, 2014.

years, the divergent voting patterns across diocesan Synods on sexuality have suggested that responses to these questions would vary significantly from diocese to diocese. There would also be major differences from congregation to congregation within dioceses: in heterogeneous Anglican dioceses such as Melbourne, there can be a marked variation in attitudes to sexual ethics across parishes, with some more progressive and some more conservative.

The same is true of the Catholic Church. There is a strong liberal strand among Catholics, but there is a strong conservative strand as well, which includes many active younger worshippers.

> Australian Catholics include a strong liberal strand and a strong conservative strand.

It is also noteworthy that in 2011, there did not seem to be a trend for younger people who attend church to adopt more permissive views on sexuality, or for older churchgoers to hold more conservative views. Indeed, the trend is the opposite: younger active Christians are more conservative, except for the 15–19-year-old cohort, who held more progressive views than 20–29-year-olds. Unfortunately, we do not have more recent data to track how the 2011 15–19-year-olds' views have developed.

The correlation noted here between progressive Christianity and ageing, declining churches is not unique to Australia. It applies throughout Western societies and has often been noted in commentary. For example, in February 2023, Christian Concern in the UK reported that when they surveyed the 33 Church of England congregations with the largest under-16 attendance, none of these churches publicly supported a change to the doctrine of marriage, and most publicly identified as opposed to embracing same-sex marriage.

Likewise, a recent global survey of Catholic women found that younger Catholic women are more opposed to same-sex marriage than older women, and the younger the cohort, the greater the opposition. The percentages of Catholic women who "strongly disagreed" with extending the sacrament of marriage to same sex couples were: Over 70 years, 7%; 56 to 70 years, 14%; 41 to 55 years, 28%; 26 to 40 years, 45%; 18 tp 25 years, 49%.[83]

In the Melbourne Anglican Diocese, where I served for over 20 years, the majority of churches with youth groups and children's programs are conservative in theology, being either evangelical or charismatic. On the other hand, children and youth are few and far between in many progressive-minded parishes.

> Children and youth are few and far between in many progressive Anglican parishes.

Some Christian advocates of same-sex marriage have argued that if the church does not embrace the prevailing culture, it will alienate younger people. For example, Steven Croft, Bishop of Oxford, expressed anxiety about what he called the looming "dislocation" between the Church of England and the surrounding society:

> In paying attention to our prevailing culture, particularly as expressed by the under forties, I am aware of their sense of this manifest unfairness, and of anger and alienation among

---

[83] *International Survey of Catholic Women: Analysis and Report of Findings*, p.52.

a whole generation. If the Church believes this clear injustice, the argument goes, then what does this say about the rest of the beliefs of the Church? Is this an organisation that is to be taken seriously at all as a moral and ethical force in the 21st century?[84]

However, evidence from around the world shows that the opposite is true: younger Christians are gravitating to the more theologically conservative churches.

These observations must be made with an important caveat. Same-sex marriage was legalised in Australia in 2017, and this will undoubtedly have had an impact on attitudes of Christians since then.

The correlation between how progressive or conservative the doctrines and ethics of a church are and that church's health, as it has manifested in the United States, has been much discussed and debated by American academics for the past half-century, since the publication in 1972 by Dean Kelly of *Why Conservative Churches are Growing: A Study in Sociology of Religion*. Potential explanations are hotly disputed. However the correlation is explained, the point is that it is real, and this must be recognised if one is to understand how Australian churches' doctrines on human sexuality may play out in the decades to come.

---

84 Steven Croft. 2022. *Together in Love and Faith: Personal Reflections and Next Steps for the Church*. Oxford: The Bishop of Oxford, p. 20.

11

LOOKING TO THE FUTURE

What does the future hold? Who is standing on the "right side of history"? Will more conservative Christian views on human sexuality inevitably, if gradually, give way to more progressive views? Or will sexually progressive versions of Christianity wither away?

> Who is standing on the "right side of history"?

NOT ALL THE SAME

Christian churches are not all the same. They vary in the depth of their histories. They also vary in the detail of their doctrinal statements. As a rule, the older the denomination, the longer and more detailed its doctrinal statement becomes, often including detailed stipulations on ethics. In younger movements, a good deal is passed on as part of the church's culture without being made explicit in written form.

For example, Pentecostal pastors would be aware that their movement rejects adultery as sinful, even if this is not inscribed in the doctrinal statements of their particular movement. Pentecostals can and do defend this view based on their movement's commitment to the authority of the Bible and its teachings on adultery, even when there is no explicit ethical statement in their doctrinal statement comparable to those found in the Catholic *Catechism* or the *Westminster Confession*.

Churches also vary in the emphasis their constituting documents put on the authority of the Bible. Consider the contrast between the Uniting Church on the one hand, whose *Basis of Union* has a weak position on Biblical authority hedged around with affirmations of human authorities, and the Catholic, Anglican, Pentecostal, and Reformed traditions on the other hand, whose views of Biblical authority are more robust.

> Churches vary in how much emphasis they put on the Bible.

Churches also differ in their capacity and willingness to apply church discipline on issues to do with human sexuality.

Catholic priests can impose discipline on lay members by excluding a person from communion ("excommunicating" them), and the Catholic Church has recently strengthened its capacity to discipline clergy. Nevertheless, its track record on dealing with sexual transgressions among the clergy has been poor.

Anglicans vary, both in what behaviours they believe need to be sanctioned—as the Perth variation to the national *Faithfulness in Service* code of conduct has shown—and in the consistency with which they impose discipline on the grounds of infringements of sexual ethics.

While the Uniting Church in Australia, which has embraced same-sex marriage, seemingly has neither the will nor the capacity to discipline pastors for adultery, the Pentecostal and Reformed churches considered here are ready to discipline for breaches of sexual ethics.

PERMISSIVE OR CONSERVATIVE?

Attitudes to sexual ethics move together in a pack. An observation from this limited survey of church polity, doctrine, and ethics is that churches that have taken steps to embrace same-sex relationships have memberships and policies that are more accepting of sex outside of marriage in general. This is apparent, for example, in the codes of conduct of both the Perth Anglican Diocese and the Uniting Church of Australia. We see a parallel pattern in surveys of members: churches in which tolerance of adultery is higher also show greater acceptance of homosexuality.

> Attitudes to sexual ethics move together in a pack.

This means that the question of same-sex marriage cannot be considered in isolation from other sexual ethics issues, including adultery and sex before marriage. Rather than classifying Christian movements in terms of being for or against same-sex marriage, it could be more accurate to classify them as being sexually permissive or conservative, and more or less influenced by the sexual revolution.

At the same time, the National Church Life Survey has shown that greater regularity in church attendance correlates with more conservative views on sexual ethics: the more committed someone is to practising their Christian faith, the more conservative their sexual ethics are likely to be.

Australian churches are parting ways over sexual ethics. On the one hand, some Australian Christian groups have been moving towards embracing more permissive views of human sexuality, including revising their positions on same-sex relationships and adultery. Examples are the Uniting Church and some, but not all, Anglican dioceses. Yet most Australian churchgoers still hold to the traditional mainstream Christian teaching that sexual relationships should be confined to heterosexual marriage. It is also clear that multiple conservative Christian denominations and movements are showing no signs of moving towards more permissive sexual ethics.

ARE CHRISTIANS EVOLVING?

We have seen that it is not the case that the whole body of Australian Christians is evolving towards more liberal views on human sexuality. Indeed, there is evidence that the opposite is true: movements that are growing and have higher concentrations of younger people tend to hold a more conservative position on sexual ethics. It is ageing, theologically progressive Christianity that is dying, while youthful, theologically conservative Christianity grows.

> Ageing, progressive Christianity is dying, while youthful conservative Christianity grows.

This suggests that sexual progressives, like the Uniting Church, will not find themselves to be on the right side of Christian history.

In the 2011 NCLS, the generation of churchgoers with the most liberal views on sexual ethics was the Baby Boomers. These were the pioneers of the sexual revolution, and this is the cohort whose influence is currently waning as they move into retirement.

Even Australia's Uniting Church, which has blazed a trail to a more liberal position on sexuality, retains a significant number of committed dissenters, so that it currently officially endorses two mutually incompatible theological positions on marriage, one progressive and one conservative. The progressives in the Uniting Church are not taking everyone with them.

The Australian Anglican Church is also divided on the issue of same-sex marriage, and it seems inevitable that its dioceses will go through a parting of the ways over this and related theological differences in the years ahead, efforts to prevent division notwithstanding.

The official teachings of the Catholic Church continue to reflect a conservative view of human sexuality, and although this seems unlikely to change, many Australian Catholic churchgoers have moved significantly to embrace more liberal views on sexual ethics. A challenge for the Catholic Church is not so much the risk of division within the denomination as how to bridge the gap between what the church teaches and what Catholics actually believe and do, while trying to stem the tide of people drifting away from active involvement.

> A challenge for the Catholic Church is how to bridge the gap between doctrine and what people actually believe and do.

The small Free Reformed Church of Australia, as a small conservative denomination in the "Other Protestant" category, teaches that human sexual expression should be confined to heterosexual marriage. This doctrinal position is apparent from its foundational documents and the proceedings of its Synod. The same is true of the Australian Presbyterian Church.

Pentecostal movements, likewise, who in terms of numbers of attenders collectively form the second-largest Australian Christian group after the Catholics, are not moving towards more liberal positions on sexuality, and they have robust discipline processes for those who breach their codes of conduct.

CHURCH DISCIPLINE

We have also seen that Christian groups that retain a more conservative position on sexual ethics also have the capacity and will to impose church discipline by decredentialing pastors who breach their codes of conduct. On the other hand, churches whose members have more liberal attitudes to sexuality may not impose church discipline on human sexuality, even when there are breaches of a code of conduct.

In the Uniting Church, adultery is no longer considered a code of conduct issue, and the Anglican Church's *Faithfulness in Service* code of conduct, which limits sexual relations to within heterosexual marriage, is not applied by some diocesan bishops, who license people living in same-sex relationships and do not necessarily withdraw the licences of clergy who commit adultery. At least one diocese, Perth, has modified the code of conduct accordingly.

It is noteworthy that although churches vary in whether they impose church discipline over sex outside heterosexual, monogamous marriage, every denomination and movement now disciplines clergy for **professional** sexual misconduct, such as sexual harassment, sexual assault, criminal sexual conduct including sexual abuse of children, and sexualisation of pastoral relationships.

For example, in the Uniting Church, where adultery is not a breach of church ethics, its *Code of Ethics and Ministry Practice* states that "Ministers shall not engage in sexual relationships with people in their professional pastoral care". The UCA only has rules for sexual ethics if it is a professional or criminal matter. They have, in effect, outsourced Christian sexual ethics to Human Relations professionals and the laws of the society around them.

> The UCA has outsourced its sexual ethics to the surrounding society.

This reinforces an observation made earlier: that the progressive trend towards embracing same-sex marriage is associated with a trend to place personal sexual ethics outside the scope of church discipline altogether. Churches that embrace same-sex marriage are more likely to accept unmarried pastors living with partners and to be more accepting of adultery. This shows that what is at stake in a shift towards same-sex marriage is not limited to attitudes to homosexuality: it affects the capacity and will of the church to speak with authority about any kind of personal sexual ethics.

In this book, I have avoided expressing an opinion on what is the "correct" Christian doctrine on human sexuality. Many have put forward arguments for a variety of views, but what is clear and indeed indisputable is that, despite some signs of movement in a few branches of Australian Christianity towards more liberal views on sexuality, the traditional Christian position is still the majority position, in terms of both the official doctrines and the opinions held by most churchgoers. Moreover, there is evidence of a generational trend towards, not away from, conservative Christian sexual ethics. Liberalisation in sexual ethics is correlated with demographic decline in churches, while church growth is correlated with more conservative sexual ethics. Similarly, churchgoers who are less committed and attend church less frequently are likely to have more permissive sexual ethics. Losing your religion and embracing the sexual revolution go hand-in-hand.

> Losing your religion and the sexual revolution go hand in hand.

A HOSTILE CLIMATE

Some secular-minded people are seeking to impose contemporary sexual ethical standards on churches and Christian organisations. The campaigns to prevent religious schools from applying a religious test in employing teachers is an example. The climate of public opinion is increasingly hostile to churches, precisely for their ethical teachings. There is an expectation among some that Christians will have to be forced to change their ways, and that the state should exert pressure through the courts to hasten this. As Andrew McGowan, then Warden of Trinity College, Melbourne and an Anglican priest of a more progressive persuasion, put it, "the churches often seem to need the courts to give them lessons".[85]

This expectation comes up against the fact that, from the earliest days of the church, Christians were known for holding views on ethics that did not align with the values of contemporary society. At the time of the Roman empire, Christians teachings on monogamy and chastity outside marriage were at odds with the culture.

---

85 Andrew McGowan. "Lessons from Christian camp's gay discrimination." *Eureka Street,* 1 May 2014. https://www.eurekastreet.com.au/article/lessons-from-christian-camp-s-gay-discrimination

LOOKING TO THE FUTURE

An increasingly challenging social and legal environment for Christians is leading some churches to protect themselves by ensuring that they have formally articulated doctrinal statements on sexual ethics. Acts Global Churches' addition of a conservative definition of marriage in their *Statement of Belief* is an example.

The more hostile legal environment will also exert pressure on churches to adhere to consistently held positions on sexual ethics, and to apply church discipline consistently as well. This will be challenging for denominations that currently embrace heterogeneous views or follow inconsistent approaches to discipline, such as the Anglican Church of Australia.

Such pressures will also push churches towards division, for to function as a single denomination implies the existence of a single, consistently applied code of ethics. Consider, for example, the situation of a theologically conservative congregation that requires its staff to adhere to a code of conduct that rejects adultery and sex outside of heterosexual, monogamous marriage. Consider what might happen if a potential staff member were denied a position with the church either because they refused to sign the code of conduct or because their sexual behaviour did not conform to the code. The person who experienced this rejection might make an anti-discrimination complaint against the church and, if the doctrine of the denomination endorsed liberal sexual ethics or if the denomination's lack of discipline allowed people to serve on the staff of other congregations in breach of the denomination's doctrine or policies, the more conservative congregation might be unable to defend its code of conduct before a tribunal. A congregation might only be safe to

> Christian teachings on sex were at odds with the culture of the Roman Empire.

uphold such a conservative code of conduct in a denomination that both holds to the same conservative views and is willing to apply church discipline accordingly.

Protections for churches to discriminate on the basis of sexual ethics will only be available when a church can show that this is done to conform to church doctrine. This protection will not be available if the official doctrine of the church does not offer this protection, or if a denomination or movement is inconsistent in applying discipline in relation to sexual ethics.

The increasing anti-discrimination pressure on churches will surely put pressure on them to have clearly defined positions on sexual ethics, and to apply discipline consistently to enforce these positions. Tolerance expressed as vagueness and inconsistency in church discipline will be increasingly untenable. Turning a blind eye to code of conduct violations will no longer be an option.

> Churches are under pressure to have clearly defined positions on sexual ethics.

As Australian churches look to their ethical statements, codes of conduct, and disciplinary processes, individual Christians are coming under increasing pressure to fall into line with societal views on human sexuality. An example was the forced resignation of Andrew Thorburn from his newly acquired role as CEO of Essendon Football Club. Thorburn had also been chair of the governing body of City on a Hill, an Anglican Church planting movement. When David Barham, the president of the football club, became aware of the views of City on a Hill pastors on abortion and homosexuality, Thorburn was immediately told to choose between his church role and his appointment at Essendon.

On resigning from Essendon, Thorburn stated, "Today, it became clear to me that my personal Christian faith is not tolerated or permitted in the public square, at least by some and perhaps by many."[86]

> "It became clear to me that my personal Christian faith is not tolerated or permitted in the public square"
>
> – Andrew Thorburn

UNEQUAL RIGHTS?

One of the issues our society faces is that the sexual revolution has not only won sexual freedoms; it has also been accompanied by a moral code that mandates respect for some sexual choices while marginalising and even inciting hatred against those who find their views to be out of step with the sexual revolution. For example, when Premier Daniel Andrews weighed in on the issue of Thorburn's appointment, he said of City on a Hill's ethical positions, "Those views are absolutely appalling. I don't support those views, that kind of intolerance, that kind of hatred, bigotry. It is just wrong."[87] Andrews went on, "To dress that up as anything other than bigotry is just obviously false." This hatred-inciting pitch, with conservative Christians in the crosshairs, must have been judged by Andrews to resonate with voters.

A problem with privileging and mandating respect for selective ethical positions as an act of inclusion is that

> Divergent views are being marginalised.

---

86   "Statement from Andrew Thorburn." https://origin.go.theaustralian.com.au/wp-content/uploads/2022/10/FILE-0273.pdf

87   https://www.afr.com/work-and-careers/leaders/andrew-thorburn-cancelled-as-essendon-ceo-after-24-hours-20221004-p5bn33

those with divergent views are marginalised and treated as objects of acceptable hatred and scorn. A conversation needs to be had about all this, but it is a conversation that Australians are manifestly ill-equipped to have. In the face of growing hostility, and with our society lacking the capacity to resolve these issues, churches must give careful thought to how they will navigate the challenging and increasingly hostile seas they find themselves in.

CONCLUSION

There is now a widespread view in Australian society that sexual ethics are a private matter. It has often been said that it is no one else's business what consenting individuals do with their bodies in the privacy of their own homes. Of course, most Christians do not actually believe this. They expect, for example, that their pastors should not commit adultery. At the same time, there are signs that the state, while asserting an individual's right to sexual freedom, is increasingly hostile to Christian beliefs about human sexuality. How will churches respond?

> The state is increasingly hostile to Christian beliefs about sex.

To return to where we started, the purpose of this short book has been to help readers understand how Christian positions on sexual ethics interact with church polity; how key decisions are made by Christian groups, including where authority lies in different traditions; and how Christian responses to the sexual revolution are likely to progress in Australia.

Roughly speaking, Australian churches are responding in three different ways to the impact of the sexual revolution.

The first category of churches rejects the outcomes of the sexual revolution, adheres to conservative Christian ethics, and applies consistent church discipline accordingly. Most Pentecostals, who form the largest Protestant movement, fall into this camp, as do some Protestant denominations. These groups will have to adapt to the more hostile social environment, but they are unlikely to change their views.

A second category of churches adheres to conservative Christian ethics in principle, but there is a gap between theory and practice which manifests as inconsistency in applying church discipline. This typically goes hand-in-hand with a substantial proportion of members holding views at odds with official teaching. For churches in this category, something will have to give.

For Catholics, a possible future is that the gap between official teaching and Catholic churchgoers' personal views could be resolved in time by a renewal of confidence in official doctrine, as a rising conservative movement amongst younger Catholics counters a drift of more liberal Catholics away from the church. This is a likely long-term outcome for the Catholic Church: its future will belong to younger conservatives, not departing ageing progressives.

Finally, there are churches who are divided on sexual ethics, including the Anglicans and the Uniting Church. The obvious and inevitable way forward for these denominations will be structural separation. In the longer term, it will simply not be sustainable for divided denominations to sustain mutually contradictory ethical approaches to sexuality. This would require contradictory disciplinary standards, an arrangement which could not be defended in the courts. Sexual ethics cannot be considered a private issue for churches, for they inform public codes of conduct for ministers and members.

The road to division will be varied, depending on the conditions that apply in the respective denominations, including their governance arrangements.

> The road to division will be varied.

For the Uniting Church, the division has, in a sense, been happening for decades, with theologically conservative members and congregations leaving in a long slow bleeding out of the denomination as the UCA has pursued its progressive path.

It also seems inevitable that Australian Anglicans will drift apart, with the fault lines appearing between the dioceses in keeping with Anglicans' episcopal polity. For individual conservative congregations that find themselves in a progressive-trending diocese, the newly formed Diocese of the Southern Cross may provide a new home.

In the category of dividing churches, there are three different mindsets shaping how individuals respond to the looming spectre of division.

Some, who would prefer to be in a first category church surrounded by others who share traditional Christian ethics, have been preparing for division. An example has been the establishment of GAFCON in Australia. However much they may at one level grieve division, people in this first category look forward to the clarity and relief they hope division will bring. They do not want to be forever debating sexual ethics at the expense of focusing on the church's mission.

> Some Christians prefer not to have to think about division at all.

LOOKING TO THE FUTURE

Some Christians prefer not to have to think or talk about division at all. They stress unity, urging everyone to focus on what could keep the church together. An example within the Anglican Church is the recently formed National Comprehensive Anglicanism Network.[88] Ultimately this "Don't mention the war" strategy seems unlikely to succeed.

Some Christians, sympathetic to a more progressive Christianity, hope that they are on the right side of history. They look forward to the Christian mainstream embracing the outcomes of the sexual revolution, including same-sex marriage. Such people often cite changes in churches' attitudes to divorce and women in ministry in the recent past, and they expect that changes in sexual ethics will follow suit.

Then there is the secular public. Some expect that Christianity will have to get in step with the world or fade away. It is even assumed by some that Christianity (and Christians) will gradually disappear from the face of the earth as more progressive views steadily displace traditionalist Christian beliefs. Sheila Jeffreys, feminist academic, made this assumption when she was younger: "I considered, like other progressive intellectuals, that religion would die out."[89]

> "I considered, like other progressive intellectuals, that religion would die out."
> – Sheila Jeffreys

---

88 Elspeth Kernebone. "New group seeks to build unity as church faces divisions." *The Melbourne Anglican*, 15 August 2023. https://tma.melbourneanglican.org.au/2023/08/new-group-seeks-to-build-unity-as-church-faces-divisions/

89 Sheila Jeffreys. 2012. *Man's Dominion: Religion and the Eclipse of Women's Rights in World Politics*. London: Routledge, pp. 1–2.

Nothing could be further from the truth. This century can be expected to live up to the label John Neuhaus gave it: "The Century of Religion".[90] While Christianity may appear spent in parts of the West, it is powering ahead across the Global South. Even in Australia, the rise of Pentecostalism, from non-existence in 1900 to being the second-largest Christian movement in the nation, contradicts the assumption of decline. Yes, Anglo-Celtic religion has been declining in Australia, but multicultural religion, including diverse expressions of Christianity, has been growing.

This book has been written to outline the complexity of how Australian churches are responding to living downstream of the sexual revolution, under the cultural dominance of expressive individualism. We have examined where authority lies in different traditions, the various ways the different traditions articulate their doctrines in writing, and their diverse approaches to the crucial issue of church discipline.

I have pointed out that it is misleading to claim that Christianity is declining in Australia. The reality is that some Christian movements and denominations have been growing while others have been declining. We have also considered correlations between sexual ethics and attendance, observing that in Australia, as elsewhere, that progressivism goes hand in hand with denominational decline. By and large, younger Australian Christians hold to more conservative views on sexual ethics than their parents, and the most sexually progressive Australian Christians are the ageing Baby Boomers.

---

90 Richard John Neuhaus. "The Approaching Century of Religion." *First Things*, October 1997. https://www.firstthings.com/article/1997/10/the-approaching-century-of-religion

We are in a period of transition. The outcome will be a parting of the ways, with divisions emerging between Christians who embrace expressive individualism with the sexual freedom it demands and those who adhere to a Biblical understanding of what it means to be human. In Australia's changing legal environment—which, it seems, will not be particularly sympathetic to Christianity—church communities will need to apply consistent church discipline, and this requirement will be a further incentive to divide, for church discipline must be grounded in a clearly articulated position on sexual ethics. Sitting on the fence will no longer be an option. The time of ambiguity, when a church could hold formally to a doctrine or principle of conduct but turn a blind eye to breaches of that doctrine or principle, is passing away.

> We are in a period of transition.

Most Christians understand that the secular people with whom they rub shoulders every day do not understand Christianity. They know that they live in a world that misunderstands them. Ignorance and misconceptions abound and we find that we have to learn to live with the resulting prejudice. Nevertheless, it is hoped that this book will do something to help dispel misconceptions. Christianity is not a fading, spent force. A great many Christians are not "evolving" to become pale projections of the culture that surrounds them. To be sure, some denominations are dying, but at the same time, others are thriving, fuelled in part by people leaving the sinking ship of progressive Christianity.

> Christians have to learn to live with prejudice against them.

Looking to the Future

It would be a mistake to see the emerging divisions in Christian churches over sexual ethics as the last throes of failing, rusted-on religious conservativism. While some Christians have been embracing the outcomes of the sexual revolution, they represent the dying fringes of Christianity, not its beating heart.

Printed in Australia
Ingram Content Group Australia Pty Ltd
AUHW020759271123
387005AU00002B/2